Landscapes of the
PYRENEES

a countryside guide
Ninth edition

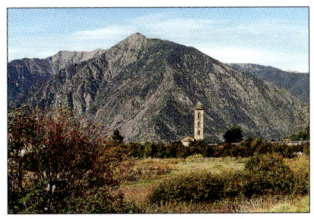

Paul Jenner and
Christine Smith

SUNFLOWER BOOKS

Ninth edition © 2025
Sunflower Books™
PO Box 36160
London SW7 3WS, UK
www.sunflowerbooks.co.uk

All rights reserved.
No part of this publication
may be reproduced, stored
in a retrieval system, or
transmitted by any form
or by any means,
electronic, mechanical,
photocopying, recording
or otherwise, without the
prior written permission
of the publishers.

Sunflower Books and
'Landscapes' are Registered
Trademarks.

ISBN 978-1-85691-568-7

Waterfalls near the Circo de Soaso (Walk 26)

Important note to the reader

We have tried to ensure that the descriptions and maps in this book are error-free at press date. The book will be updated, where necessary, whenever future editions are printed. It is very helpful for us to receive your comments (sent to info@sunflowerbooks.co.uk, please) for the updating of future editions.

We also rely on walkers to take along a good supply of common sense — as well as this book — on their rambles. **Be aware that the category of difficulty for any walk, most especially in the central and western Pyrenees, can change dramatically according to weather conditions.** A walk in the central Pyrenees that is easy in high summer could be impossible in spring due to snow. A route in the western Pyrenees, easily found one day, may call for skilled compass or GPS work in heavy mist the next. If the route is not as we outline it, and your way ahead is not secure, return to the point of departure. ***Never attempt to complete a tour or walk under hazardous conditions!*** Please read carefully the notes on pages 38 to 44, as well as the introductory comments at the beginning of each tour and walk (regarding road conditions, equipment, grade, distances and time, etc). Explore *safely*, while at the same time respecting the beauty of the countryside.

Cover: griffon vulture above Ordesa's canyon (Walk 22)
Title page: Sant-Miquel d'Engolasters and the mountains of Andorra (Walk 11)
Photographs pages 2, 108, 114-115, 116-117, 125, 132-133: Neil Hardy; pages 1, 8-9, 10-11, 13, 14, 15, 17 (bottom), 18-19, 20 (top), 22, 24, 47, 49, 56-57 (bottom), 65, 74, 75, 81 (bottom): John Underwood; 2, 20 (bottom), 45, 51, 67, 70, 84-5, 87, 88-9, 92-3, 96-7, 111, 128 (top), 129 and cover: Shutterstock; all other photographs: the authors
Drawings by John Theasby
Maps: Nick Hill for Sunflower Books. Base map data © OpenStreetMap contributors. Contour data made available under ODbL (opendatacommons.org/licenses/odbl/1.0)
A CIP catalogue record for this book is available from the British Library.
Printed and bound in England: Short Run Press, Exeter

Contents

Preface	5
Pyrenees — the people	6
Acknowledgements; Books	6
Getting about	7
Picnicking	8
Touring	10
Car tour 1: **THE ALBERES**	12
Car tour 2: **INTO THE MOUNTAINS**	14
Car tour 3: **TO THE CADI**	16
Car tour 4: **THE PLATEAU OF THE CATHARS**	18
Car tour 5: **DEEP VALLEYS, HIGH PEAKS, PAINTED CAVES**	21
Car tour 6: **PARC NACIONAL D'AIGÜES TORTES**	23
Car tour 7: **'GROTTES' AND GARGOYLES**	25
Car tour 8: **MARVELS AND MIRACLES**	27
Car tour 9: **GRAND CANYONS TOUR**	29
Car tour 10: **THE VALLEY OF THE BEAR**	31
Car tour 11: **LIMESTONE AND LEGENDS**	33
Car tour 12: **INTO THE BASQUE COUNTRY**	35
Country code for walkers and motorists	37
Walking (● see explanation of symbols on page 38)	38
Weather	38
Transport	39
Clothing and equipment	39
Food and water	40
Waymarking, maps and grading of the walks	40
Safety and guides	41
Organisation of the walks	42
Overnight accommodation	43
Language hints	43
WALKS IN THE EASTERN PYRENEES	
● 1 From Vilajuïga to Llançà	45
● 2 From Cadaqués to Roses	48
● 3 From Collioure to Banyuls-sur-Mer	51
● 4 Circuit in the Garrotxa, and Santa Pau	55
● 5 Sant Aniol d'Aguja	58
● 6 Alta Garrotxa and Santa Bàrbara de Pruneres	61
● 7 A Canigou canter	63
● 8 Carança cliffhanger	65
● 9 From Núria to Queralbs	68
● 10 Pedraforca	71

4   Landscapes of the Pyrenees

WALKS IN THE CENTRAL PYRENEES
- 11 Engolasters and the Madriu Valley — 74
- 12 Mourgouillou Valley and the lakes — 77
- 13 Gorgeous Gorges de la Frau — 80
- 14 Among the lakes — 82
- 15 Circuit around Lake Artax (Artats) — 84
- 16 Crête des Isards — 86
- 17 Parc Nacional d'Aigüestortes — 88
- 18 A taste of the Baronnies — 90
- 19 The roof of the Pyrenees — 93
- 20 Cirque de Gavarnie — 95
- 21 Russell's Caves — 98
- 22 Brèche de Roland — 100
- 23 Circuit from the Pont d'Espagne via the Vallée du Marcadau and Lac du Pourtet — 103
- 24 Valle de Pineta and Punta del Valle — 106
- 25 The Añisclo Canyon — 109
- 26 Ordesa — the grand canyon walk — 111
- 27 Pic d'Anie — 115

WALKS IN THE WESTERN PYRENEES
- 28 The song of Roland (Mt Astobizkar) — 118
- 29 Roncesvalles — 120
- 30 Iparla Ridge — 122
- 31 Circuit based on Biriatou — 125
- 32 Xoldokogaina (Choldokogagna) — 129
- 33 Col d'Ibardin — 131
- 34 Peñas de Aia (Aiako Harria) — 132

Index of place names — 135
Fold-out Pyrenees map — *inside back cover*

Plateau de Sault

Preface

Words on a page work a strange magic. Words like Albères, Sault, Cadí, Ordesa, Brèche, Ossoue, Vignemale, Iparla, and Aspe may be meaningless to you today but, once you have experienced the tours and walks in this book, they will ever after disturb your sleep. Perhaps your days, too.

The Albères ... the hot sun of the Mediterranean, shady forests of cork oak, dolmens and vineyards. Plateau de Sault ... where birds of prey fill the sky, and the agricultural life of the Middle Ages can still be tasted. Cadí ... so remotely beautiful that life in a town may never be palatable again. Ordesa ... sheer canyon walls and on them the shadow of the lammergeier, Europe's largest vulture. Brèche ... the freedom of a high mountain frontier crossing. Ossoue ... where marmots fight to the death. Vignemale ... the last great glacier of the Pyrenees. Iparla ... the adrenalin rush of a spectacular ridge walk.

Some other words have the power to make you sad. Aspe and Ordesa, where the last Pyrenean brown bears and the last Pyrenean ibex were hunted to extinction. (Happily both species have now been reintroduced.) Throughout this book we try to emphasise the environment in which you will be driving, walking and picnicking, because if that is not enjoyed by you and many others, there will be no force for its preservation. If you feel, as we do, that the wilderness of the Pyrenees is important, we hope you will add your voice to those who argue for conservation — for the lammergeier, the izard, the brown bear and, above all, for the habitat itself, without which no schemes for the conservation of individual species can have any chance of success.

Landscapes of the Pyrenees is principally a guide to the outdoors, but we have not neglected the work of man. In particular, the prehistoric remains, which include some of the most important painted caves in the world and a large number of dolmens, seem to us to be very much a part of the natural world that early man inhabited.

The book is divided into three main sections, each with its own introduction.

For **motorists** there are twelve car tours, all designed to give you a taste of the huge geographical diversity that, in the Pyrenees, can exist within a very small area.

For **walkers** there are sixty long and short walks described in detail — some classics, some devised by ourselves — all chosen for their combination of superb scenery, wildlife, and historical and human interest.

For **picnickers** we have chosen a number of sites, both organised and 'wild' (for those who like a generous helping of *al fresco* with their cheese sarnies). All sites operate a *take-away* service — that is, you take away all your debris!

Enjoy the Pyrenees!

Pyrenees — the people

With its mountain domain stretching virtually coast-to-coast, there is a wide diversity of Pyrenean stock. In the west are the Basques with their immaculately white-washed homes, pink *frontons* and a curious language. In the east are the Catalans with their stone-built *masias* (farmhouses) and slightly more recognisable language (halfway between Spanish and French). But a common factor of all these mountain people is a changing lifestyle. Although there are a few souls still forging an agricultural living from the high pastures, there is a new generation of mountain entrepreneur — shepherding tourists and husbanding giant hydroelectric projects in the shadow of the peaks.

Acknowledgements

We are indebted to the following for help in researching this book:

Marti Pujol i Gou of the Ajuntament in Vilabertran for his tireless pursuit of prehistoric remains in Spain's Alt Empordà;

Jean-Marc Abadie for lifting our sights above road level to discover the extraordinary life on the enchanted mountain of Pibeste;

Toby Oliver of Brittany Ferries for advice on walks in countryside directly accessed from the company's Plymouth-Santander service;

Jean-Louis Trescazes and the village of Gavarnie;

Neil and Rossella Hardy, proprietors of the outdoor equipment shop Telemark Pyrenees in Ax-les-Thermes, for updating the west coast walks and researching Walks 15 and 23.

Books

It should be emphasised that *Landscapes of the Pyrenees* is a guide to countryside exploration and should be used in conjunction with a standard guide such as the *Rough Guide to the Pyrenees*. More walks and tours in and around the Pyrenees can be found in other Sunflower 'Landscapes' guides: *Basque Regions of Spain and France*; *Costa Brava and Barcelona*; *Languedoc-Roussillon and Western Provence*. Also of interest is *Wild Spain* (Sierra Club), especially for its coverage of surviving wildlife and wilderness.

Marmot

Getting about

This is a countryside guide to *all* of the Pyrenees — to the wild and haunting scenery in France, Spain and Andorra, stretching some 400km between the Mediterranean and the Atlantic. Some of the tours and walks are entirely within one country, but many take you across borders — so a passport in your pocket is a good idea, even though formal frontier checks no longer exist.

Unless you have a great deal of time, such scale demands a **car**. If you fly in, hire is easy throughout the Pyrenees, with rates generally a little cheaper in Spain — especially if you can make the most of a package deal. Petrol, diesel and EV charging are also a little cheaper in Spain, but cheapest of all is Andorra. (Don't forget your driving licence, valid insurance, vehicle registration document, and, if you are taking your own car, two warning triangles, reflective safety jackets, spare bulbs, fire extinguisher, first aid kit and a GB sticker. In France you should also carry a self-test breathalyser.)

There are several useful **train** services, particularly those along the Mediterranean and Atlantic coastal strips and in the northern foothills. These include the Perpignan/Cerdagne line with its Petit Train Jaune segment from Villefranche to La Tour de Carol, and the Paris/Toulouse/Barcelona service which also stops at La Tour de Carol, giving access to Andorra and to the rack railway into the mountains at Núria.

Buses vary in their usefulness to the walker, since the timetables are often designed for locals coming down into the towns in the mornings and returning in the evenings. We suggest a number of the more regular services.

Coach tours can be a way of seeing the countryside and sometimes getting to walks, particularly for popular beauty spots such as Gavarnie and the Pont d'Espagne — or for shopping expeditions to Andorra.

Taxis, and their more rugged mountain counterparts, the **jeep-taxis**, will have to be used on some occasions by those who have no car, for example in the Parc Nacional d'Aigües Tortes and to get to the Barrage d'Ossoue for Walk 21.

At the beginning of every walk we give details of the public transport services available and provide a telephone number or web address for up-to-date information. If you cannot speak the language, contact the local tourist office or ask your hotel to make enquiries.

🌻 Picnicking

Official picnic sites are few and far between in the Pyrenees and often, where they do exist, they are *too* accessible (just beside a main road for example) and may be sadly littered, when compared with 'wilder' sites. We have deliberately restricted suggested picnic spots on the grounds that virtually the entire Pyrenean range is one wonderful picnic setting. However we have included a specific suggestion or two at the top of each car tour, for those who enjoy a little company in their *al fresco* dining rooms; see the '*P*' symbols on the maps.

Please try to take your own litter away with you — even where there are bins provided, these inevitably attract more donations than they can contain, with unpleasant results. And tidying up your deposit in a plastic bag is not the answer. We are always aware of crossing a mountain frontier even without the benefit of customs — in France they sling their bright blue plastic refuse bags, but in Spain the rubbish is less 'tidy'.

Fires: Never light a fire other than in one of the fireplaces provided at organised picnic sites. The Pyrenees have suffered some devasting bush fires over the years.

Picnicking

Eats: If cooking is going to be difficult — don't. Feast instead on the wide variety of continental cheeses, meats and of course breads which are readily available in the mountains. Buy your bread in good time — bearing in mind that in France many *boulangeries* close at 13.00 sharp, and in Spain many will remain closed for most of the afternoon. Even the largest supermarkets usually have a lengthy lunch-break, which can prove disastrous for the ravenous traveller.

Water: Drinking fountains *(fonts)* should be fine. Many mountain streams are not only safe, they are delicious — if you use common sense: never drink still or sluggish water; avoid any rivers where there is luxuriant water-weed growth or obvious pollution. Check your map to see if there is habitation above your stream, even a refuge or *cabane*. Avoid the water if there are plentiful signs of animals.

Once again we advise common sense in your dress — that is, sturdy shoes for walking, cover-ups, sunhat and, particularly in high mountain areas, sunglasses (the glare can be fierce).

All picnickers should read the country code on page 37 and go quietly in the countryside.

Car tour 3: At Maçaners you have this astounding view to Pedraforca — the forked rock — landmark of the Cadí.

☀ Touring

In the Pyrenees remote scenery can be enjoyed without even getting out of your car, especially if you are willing to drive on tracks. The Añisclo Canyon, the Yaga, the Cadí, Canigou — these and many more are places where a feeling of wilderness is preserved, despite access by road. Unfortunately that remoteness is under threat, especially on the Spanish side of the range, where EU money is helping to fund major road development.

Progress along the foothills of the Pyrenees is admittedly slow. You can drive coast-to-coast via the French motorway system in an afternoon, but to travel closer to the peaks means a traverse of three days *minimum*.

Because of the relative remoteness of many areas, there may be no snow clearance in winter on some passes. It may be June before some minor roads are open to traffic, and these may be closed again from November onwards, due to winter storms. If you are touring in early or late season, be sure to carry snow chains (available at low cost in supermarkets in France and Spain), or be prepared to modify your plans according to conditions.

The 12 tours in this book give a comprehensive picture of the entire range. The touring notes are brief: they include little

Touring

history or information readily available in other publications. *We concentrate instead on route-planning:* each tour is designed to give you an introduction to scenery in a particular part of the Pyrenees and to provide as much variety as possible. We want to show you our favourite landscapes in the Pyrenees *and take you to the starting point of some delightful* **walks.**

If you are touring, consider spending the night en route, rather than trying to rush back to base. Several tours cross frontiers — so although formal frontier checks are a thing of the past you should always have your passport with you. Your car documentation (see 'Getting about') should also be in the vehicle at all times.

The fold-out touring map is designed to be held out opposite the touring notes and contains, in a handy compact form, all the planning information you need to follow our suggested tours. Due to its small scale, you may wish to buy a more detailed map; if so, we can recommend 'Pyrenean Region' (Freytag-Berndt; scale 1:400,000). For even more detail, Michelin covers the range in three 1:150,000 maps. Note also: our map only shows those tracks that we have driven ourselves and found to be suitable for the majority of cars. Moreover, we suggest alternative tarmac roads for the owners of exceptionally large vehicles (or Porsches!). Average speed on tracks will not exceed 30kph/18mph.

Lack of space prevents us from printing town plans, so we give you clear guidance through all built-up areas in the touring notes. However, if you will be spending any length of time in the Pyrenees, you will need to rely on your smart phone to navigate the towns — or carry up-to-date Michelin hotel guides for France and Spain, with their wealth of town plans

The symbols used in the touring notes correspond to those on the pull-out map; see map key.

All motorists should read the country code on page 37 and go quietly in the countryside.

A typical village of the eastern Pyrenees — Eus, near Prades and an access road to Canigou for Walk 7

Car tour 1: THE ALBERES

La Jonquera • Vilajuïga • Roses • Port de la Selva • Llançà • Portbou • Cerbère • Banyuls-sur-Mer • Port-Vendres • Collioure • Argelès • Le Boulou

134km/83mi; about 5 hours' driving, starting on the motorway at Junction 2 (La Jonquera) and finishing on the motorway at Le Boulou.
Walks en route or nearby: 1-3
A tour accessible from anywhere on the Costa Brava, by joining the coastal toll-motorway A7/E15 and taking Exit 2 (La Jonquera) on the Spanish side of the frontier. The circuit combines the archaeologically and historically rich plains of the Alt Empordà with a long, twisty and consistently-attractive coastal drive, also providing the opportunity to compare Spanish and French wines, direct from the producers.
Picnic suggestions: Some 7km beyond **Vilajuïga**, on the road to Sant Pere de Rodes you will see, on the right, **Mas Ventós** (⌱) — a picnic area with ample parking. Tables and benches are shaded by pine trees with outstanding views southwards across the Bay of Roses. An excellent spot to meet up with friends doing Walk 1; see map pages 46-47. Further on along the intinerary, once on the coast, choose any beach that grabs your fancy. Your choice includes: **Llançà, Portbou, Cerbère, Banyuls-sur-Mer, Port-Vendres, Collioure** or **Argelès**. Sheltered coves or wide stretches of sand, plenty of nearby refreshment and WC facilities.

If you don't object to a long day, this tour gives you the chance to make some interesting detours and perhaps take a swim at one of the popular resorts along the Côte Vermeille.

Take EXIT 2 (LA JONQUERA) off the AP7-E15 motorway, turning right (south) onto the N11, following signs for FIGUERES. After 7km/4.5mi turn left onto the GI602 (signposted 'CAPMANY, ESPOLLA'). You are now on the 'wine and olive oil route' where every village has its *co-operativa*. Stop and taste at **Capmany**, **Espolla**, **Garriguella**, **Vilajuïga** and **Pau**.

From Sant Climent an excursion is possible to the castle of Requesens, while from Garriguella you could make a short detour to the castle/casino of Perelada (■). Just beyond Garriguella you can, if you wish, shorten the tour by turning left on the N260, direct to Llançà. We continue straight ahead, to **Vilajuïga**, where Walk 1 begins. *(From here you have the option of visiting Sant Pere de Rodes and the Mas Ventós picnic area — a detour of 14km return; see map pages 46-47.)*

The main tour continues straight ahead on the GI610 for **Roses** (36km/22mi ▲△✕⃝WC), the largest resort on this stretch of the Costa Brava, at the north end of an immense curve of sand.

From Roses take the GI614 up and over the mountains to PORT DE LA SELVA. *(From the summit, 12km beyond Roses, you have the option of another detour — to Cadaqués, a picturesque and very different resort, made famous by the Catalan surrealist painter Salvador Dalí. Allow 10km return.)*

From **Port de la Selva** (56km/35mi ▲△✕⃝WC) you will now follow the coastal corniche to France. *(Just outside the village, a turning on the left presents you with a second opportunity to detour to Sant Pere de Rodes and Mas Ventós.)* After 6km, **Llançà** (62km/38.5mi

The rose-coloured dome of the church is clearly visible as we climb above Collioure on Walk 3.

🏨△✕🅿WC) lies a little inland of its fishing port, an ancient defensive measure against pirates. Walk 1 ends here.

From here the road to France (N260) is increasingly spectacular. The tunnels make this a pleasurable journey even in busy peak season, with fresh vistas at regular intervals. We follow the coast to **Colera** (△) and then climb steeply past rocky bays, some with their architect-designed homes, others so rugged that not even the most enterprising developer has yet had his way. Enjoy wonderful views of open sea and sheltered coves back to the Cadaqués Peninsula and Cap de Créus and ahead to the frontier at Cerbère.

There is a steep, bird's-eye view descent (📷) into **Portbou** (76km/47mi 🏨🏠✕🅿WC), the final beach resort on the Costa Brava and a major rail terminus, before the road climbs again past the last petrol station in Spain to the frontier (🅿; open 08.00 to 20.00 in summer and from 09.00 to 13.00, then 14.00 to 19.00 in winter).

Your road is now called the D914 and winds uphill and down for 4km to the attractive port of **Cerbère** (83km/52mi 🏨🏠✕🅿 WC), the rail terminus on the French side of the border, its network of bridges and viaducts providing a perfect setting for cops-and-robbers film chases.

At **Peyrefite**, between Cerbère and Banyuls, you can follow the underwater nature trail in the marine reserve — bring your snorkling gear. Notice too, that the viniculture is far more intensive than on the Spanish side (photo on page 51). **Banyuls-sur-Mer★** (94km/58mi 🏨🏠△✕🅿WC), birthplace of sculptor Aristide Maillol (photo on page 54), is a fashionable resort. Walk 3 ends here — as does the French traverse of the Pyrenees.

Continue along the coast to **Port-Vendres** (102km/63mi 🏨🏠✕🅿WC), a major fishing harbour, and **Collioure★** (105km/65mi 🏨🏠△✕🅿✝🏛MWC), where Walk 3 begins. In the summer of 1905 Matisse and Derain set up their easels in the village and painted the brightly-coloured images that garnered them the title of 'Fauves' or 'wild beasts'. Be sure to visit Les Templiers café on Quai de l'Amirauté, by the Château Royal, where the walls are covered in paintings by the many artists who have worked in the area. (You can also see some pen and inks by Matisse in the modern art museum in Céret — Car tour 2.)

From Collioure the road climbs up the last headland, leaving the Côte Vermeille behind and dropping down to the huge flat sweep of the Côte Radieuse resorts, beginning with **Argelès-sur-Mer★** (112km/69mi 🏨🏠△✕🅿MWC). From here you can take the main D618 back to the motorway at Le Boulou, but we recommend the more picturesque D2 among the northern foothills and vineyards of the Pyrenees to **Sorède** (119km/74mi), and then **Laroque des Albères** (122km/76mi △), followed by the D11 to **Montesquieu** (126km/78mi) and on to **Le Boulou** (134km/83mi 🏨🏠✕🅿) and the motorway.

Car tour 2: INTO THE MOUNTAINS

Girona • Banyoles • Besalú • Olot • Ripoll • Sant Joan de les Abadesses • Camprodon • Prats-de-Molló • Amélie-les-Bains • Céret • Le Boulou

183km/115mi; about 6 hours' driving.
Walks en route or nearby: 4-9
An all-day circular tour, beginning and ending on the motorway, and therefore easily accessible to visitors from anywhere along the Côte Vermeille/Costa Brava, this excursion includes some of the most important historical sites in the eastern Pyrenees and some very spectacular scenery — in both France and Spain.
Picnic suggestion: At **Banyoles** follow signs for 'Estany (Lake) de Banyoles' (⌐). Limited benches and tables available; the picnic area is signposted.

The Pyrenees of history and pre-history provides the theme for this tour — Banyoles, with the remains of pre-Neanderthal Man, up to 200,000 years old; Besalú with its ancient Jewish quarter; Ripoll, founded by Wilfred 'the Shaggy'; and Sant Joan de les Abadesses, home of his daughter. Take time, too, to walk around the attractive walled town of Prats-de-Molló.

Leave the AP7 motorway at JUNCTION 6 FOR 'GIRONA NORTH' and then follow signs to **Banyoles★** (18km/11mi ⛰️🏠△✕🅿️✝M). Either skirt the pretty — though usually crowded — lake around the western shore (follow signs for 'ESTANY'; ⌐), or continue to Besalú directly by the main road along the eastern shore. (If you are already familiar with Besalú, a third option is to take the road to Mieres and Santa Pau instead. This is a slow but fascinating route through the heart of the Garrotxa (pronounced Garrocha), the volcanic region illustrated in the photos on pages 56-57 (Walk 4). You would rejoin the main tour at Olot.) At **Besalú★** (32km/20mi ✝🏛️🏠✕🅿️) stop to walk across the old bridge shown below and inside the walls of this living museum, before taking the A26 westwards.

Just before **Castellfollit de la Roca★** (✝✕🏛️M) turn off for Montagut and Sadernes if you want to do Walk 5 or 6. Continuing on, you can bypass Castellfollit via the

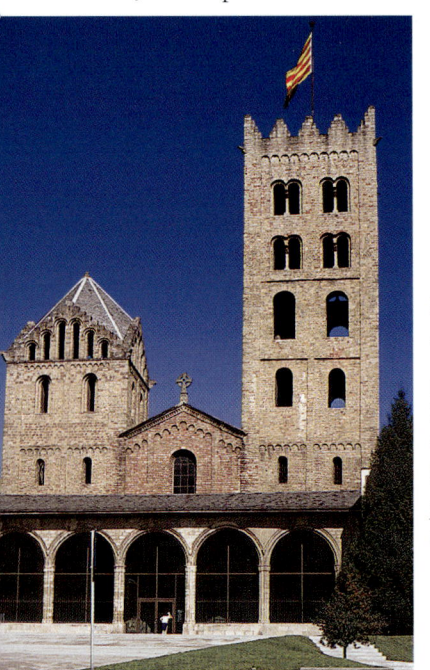

Left: The Monasterio de Santa María at Ripoll; above: the bridge at Besalú

Canigou from the north

spectacular bridge and tunnels, but we recommend you go in to see the old houses perched dramatically on sheer basalt cliffs over the River Fluvià. At night, floodlights emphasise the fluted rock.

Olot★ (52km/32mi 🏨🏛△✕🚗M) can also be bypassed, but the Museu Comarcal is worth seeing, for its collection of *Olot School* painters. Parking for Walk 4 is some 3.5km southeast of the town, at Can Serra on the GI524 towards Santa Pau.

The main tour continues from Olot towards VALLFOGONA on the N260a, the alternative 'scenic' route to Ripoll, along a road which climbs dramatically through tree-drenched hills to the **Coll de Caubet** (1010m/3310ft 📷), where there are magnificent views north and south. Beyond **Vallfogona** (🏨🚗), **Ripoll**★ (85km/53mi ✝🏨△✕🚗WC) is an essential stop for its Monasterio de Santa María, founded in 879 by Wilfred the Shaggy.

Readers using the car tour as a stepping-stone to the west can now continue on the N260 to Ribes de Freser (and Walk 9); otherwise leave Ripoll on the C26/N260 for **Sant Joan de les Abadesses**★ (✝🏨🏛✕🚗MWC), one of the most remarkable sights of the area and home of Wilfred's daughter, Emma, who founded an important monastery in the 9th century.

Continue to the small mountain town of **Camprodon**★ (112km/70mi 🏨🏛△✕🚗WC), birthplace of the Catalan composer Isaac Albéniz. From here climb steeply — we almost ran off the road once when we spotted the rare short-toed eagle — to the **Col d'Ares** (1513m/4965ft 📷), bleak despite its relatively low height. The road then descends just as steeply to **Prats-de-Molló**★ (144km/90mi 🏨🏛△✕🚗WC) with its fortified walls and huge square, frequently the scene of *boules* tournaments.

You are now in the **Tech Valley**, a region also known as the Vallespir, with the magnificent Canigou massif to the north. The **Gorges de la Fou** are on the outskirts of **Arles-sur-Tech** (164km/102mi 🏨🏛✕) — worth visiting, but see also Tour 4 for gorges you don't have to pay for! Continue along the Tech Valley by the D115 to the busy spa town of **Amélie-les-Bains**★ (167km/104mi 🏨🏛△✕🚗WC). Those wanting to ascend Canigou or the Carança should cross the Tech by the *second* bridge, to get on the D618 (signed to 'Montbolo') and at the Col Xatard take the D13 (to Valmanya for Walk 7, to the D66 for Walk 8). Some 8km beyond Amélie, turn right into **Céret**★ (🏨🏛✕🚗M) to see the collection of paintings by the Fauves and others (mentioned in Car tour 1). Then return to the D115 and rejoin the motorway near **Le Boulou** (183km/115mi).

Car tour 3: TO THE CADÍ

Andorra la Vella • La Seu d'Urgell • Bellver • Llívia • Túnel del Cadí • Guardiola • Saldes • Gósol • Tuixén • La Seu d'Urgell • Andorra la Vella

210km/130mi; about 5 hours' driving.
Walks en route or nearby: 8-11
One of the most beautiful car tours in this book, passing along the dramatic north face of the Serra del Cadí and then plunging into the very heart of the Cadí-Moixeró Parc Natural.
Picnic suggestions: There are two especially good organised picnic sites in the Cadí, near the setting for Walk 10. Just west of **Saldes** you will see signs for the 'REFUGI LLUÍS ESTASEN'. Drive up this track, to see another sign on your left: 'LA SERRA AREA RECREATIVA 2,5KM'. Bear left at the first fork and continue uphill to the picnic sites (⊼; full facilities including barbecues and WC). The **Mirador de Gresolet**, with wonderful views over the Serra del Cadí, is not far beyond the picnic areas. From **Gósol** take the road towards TUIXÉN and after 2.3km/1.4mi follow a track to the right, signposted 'FONT TERRERS' (⊼). Continue for a further 0.7km/0.4mi. Here, on a shoulder, in a delightful setting with views of the Serra del Cadí, are tables, benches, barbecue. See map on page 71.

This tour is a favourite of ours on account of its old stone buildings, its magnificent mountains, riverside picnic spots, and fabulous colour scheme (you'll see what we mean!). You will visit some 'forgotten' villages, where time has stood still.

If you are staying in **Andorra la Vella★** (♦︎▲▲▲✕♥WC; Walk 11) or nearby, take the CG1 south* to the border, where the road becomes the N145, and continue to La Seu d'Urgell (other readers join this circular route at the most convenient point). At the approach to **La Seu d'Urgell★** (21km/13mi ♦︎▲▲▲△✕♥M) turn left on the N260, following signs to 'BARCELONA/TÚNEL DEL CADÍ'.

As you drive along the broad and luxuriant **Segré Valley**, the dramatic north faces of the Cadí summits are on your right — you will be returning through the Cadí later in the day. *(After 24km you come to a left turn to Lles (45km/28mi), a famous viewpoint (☞) which you could visit as an 18km return detour.)*

The main tour continues for another 3km to the attractive hilltop village of **Bellver de Cerdanya** (48km/30mi △✕). Continue towards PUIGCERDA and, 3km beyond Bellver, ignore the turning right for the Túnel del Cadí, keeping on the N260 (but if you wish to do a short-cut and miss Llívia, taking this right turn will save 35km/22mi). At the roundabout in front of the border post at **Puigcerda★** (66km/41mi ♦︎▲▲▲✕♥WC) take the **Llívia★** (71km/44mi ♦︎▲▲▲✕♥M) exit, soon entering this historic Spanish enclave in France. From here you could continue east to the D66, to reach Walk 8, but the main tour returns to Puigcerda (76km/47mi). Follow signs before and through **Alp** for the TÚNEL DEL

---

*You may prefer to leave Andorra la Vella and head first towards France, via the **Port d'Envalira**. The road climbs through magnificent scenery to the highest road pass in the Pyrenees (2048m). There is also the option of the Envalira tunnel, the highest tunnel in Europe (2052m). Once over the border and onto the N20, head south for **Bourg-Madame** and **Puigcerda**, where you can pick up the main tour.

CADÍ. (Or, for Walk 9, turn left before Alp on the N260 for *RIPOLL*.)

The **Túnel del Cadí** (94km/58mi; a charge is made) is over 5km long and takes you under the high peaks of the Cadí to emerge near **Greixer** (102km/63mi). Continue on the main C16 to **Guardiola** (108km/67mi ♦✕♛). Some 1km beyond Guardiola turn right (signposted *'SALDES'*). After crossing the Saldes River, the road winds up to a shelf along the southern edge of the **Parc Natural Cadí-Moixeró**. At **Maçaners** (Massanes) you have the wonderful view (📷) of **Pedraforca** shown on pages 8-9 — the twin-peaked mountain that is as much a symbol of the region as the park's official black woodpecker. Beyond **Saldes** (126km/78mi ♦△✕♛⊟) the landscape is increasingly 'Wild West', with red-rock gulches (📷).

Walk 10 ascends Pedraforca from **Gósol** (136km/84mi ♦♦✕⊟; photos on pages 72-73). This little village inspired the young Picasso, and a plaque on a house in the Plaça Major (square) commemorates his stay. You are now in the heart of the park, with a good chance of spotting izards (especially if you follow Walk 10), red and roe deer, partridges and golden eagles.

Beyond Gósol the road climbs to the **Coll de Josa** (1625m/5330ft 📷), where there is a panoramic view of the Serra del Cadí and its highest peak, the Canal Baridana (2642m/8665ft). As you drop down to the Josa River and the engaging hilltop village of **Josa del Cadí** shown above, you are deep in the park. At **Tuixén** (150km/93mi ✝♦✕) turn left over the bridge to explore the village, otherwise follow signposts to *'LA SEU D'URGELL'*.

The road now continues past a succession of old stone-built villages — **Cornellana**, **Fórnols**, and **Adraén**, just beyond which the road begins to descend northwards, opening up views towards Andorra ahead and along the spectacular north face of the Cadí behind. Finally the road drops down into the Segre Valley back at **La Seu** (189km/117mi), from where you can return to **Andorra la Vella** (210km/130mi).

View south to the Serra del Cadí from the N260 east of La Seu d'Urgell; above: Josa del Cadí

Car tour 4: THE PLATEAU OF THE CATHARS

Tarascon-sur-Ariège • Col de Marmare • (Montaillou) • Comus • Pas de l'Ours • Plateau de Sault • L'Espine • Montségur • Roquefixade • Foix • Tarascon-sur-Ariège

135km/84mi; about 4 hours' driving
Walks en route or nearby: 12-16
This circular tour, which begins and ends at Tarascon-sur-Ariège, visits one of the most remote regions in France, the last medieval stronghold of the Christian religious sect known as the Cathars — 'the pure ones'. It includes a section on good, but very narrow track, which is not recommended for nervous motorists. (To avoid this, after visiting the Pas de l'Ours, return to the D613 and head east, then take the D29 north to La Bénague.) If approaching the region from the south, it may be more convenient to join the tour by taking the road out of Ax-les-Thermes that climbs up to the Col de Chioula via Ignaux. **Note:** *Between the main centres there is little in the way of petrol or refreshments.*
Picnic suggestions: From **Comus** the 'Route des Sapins' leads to the Col de la Gargante (3km), the **Pas de l'Ours** (3.6km) and an 'Aire de Picnic' (10km). See caption below and map on page 80.

Birds — some of them quite rare — outnumber human residents in this remote area of the Pyrenees. Below ground, pot-holers are in their element. But apart from ornithologists and speleologists, this tour offers exciting vistas for the ordinary motorist, including an impressive canyon.

From **Tarascon-sur-Ariège** (▲▲▲ ✕🅿; Walks 14-16) drive north on the D618 and, after the village of **Bompas** (3km/2mi), take a right turn onto the D20 (signposted 'ARNAVE' and 'COL DE MARMARE'). The narrow road climbs to magnificent views of the **Ariège Valley**, at **Axiat** passing below the talc quarry at Trimouns. Carry on to the **Col de Marmare** (1361m/ 4465ft; 36km/22mi), where the road joins the D613 coming up from Ax-les-Thermes. (If you are taking any walkers to Mérens-les-Vals, where Walk 12 begins, turn right here: Mérens lies some 8km south of Ax-les-Thermes on the N20.)

You are now on the edge of a huge and wild plateau, one of the least known corners of France, where vultures, buzzards and kestrels soar and dive for prey and sometimes simply play, happy to

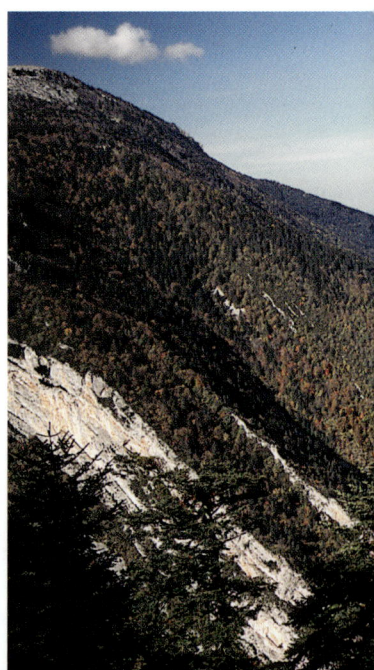

The Pas de l'Ours, with its wonderfully vertiginous view over the Gorges de la Frau (Walk 13), is a splendid picnic spot. But there is nowhere to park. Park at the Col de la Gargante and walk the 600m to this pass (see map on page 80).

ignore the passing motorist … unless you stop. Then they are off. You can see your narrow road snaking ahead for miles.

Just beyond **Prades** (40km/25mi ⛺▲✕🅿WC) reach the turning left for **Comus** (43km/27mi ▲), the starting point for Walk 13. *(Not far beyond the Comus junction, a turn-off on the right leads to Montaillou, once an important village for the Cathars. If you visit Montaillou, double back and return to Comus.)*

Continue through Comus on the D20, signposted 'ROUTE DES SAPINS'. The road gives way to track, which is reassuringly wide at first. Some 3km from Comus you reach a junction at the **Col de la Gargante**, where there is ample parking. Beyond this point the track becomes very narrow. If you are taking the alternative route (D613/D29), first park and walk to the Pas de l'Ours, to enjoy the view shown below.

Whether by car or on foot, at the col *ignore* the track turning sharp right; *ignore also* the track straight ahead signed 'Point de vue 0,7km'. Take, instead, the level track to the left signposted 'ROUTE DES SAPINS'; in 600m it brings you to one of the most awesome views in Europe at the **Pas de l'Ours** (📷), where there is a 600m/1970ft sheer drop into the Gorges de la Frau (Walk 13).

From here the single-lane track follows a narrow well-wooded ledge, with unprotected edges, but driving is easy … *unless you meet someone coming from the opposite direction*. After stopping to see the view, continue on the track, which descends past a small forest refuge and then swings away from the gorge. Some 6km beyond the Pas de l'Ours come to a sign denoting the end of the '**Forêt Domaniale de la Plaine et de Comus**', where another track joins from the right (from Belcaire). Continue until you reach another divide: here ignore 'Aire de picnic 200 metres' signposted to the left (unless you want to stop at an organised picnic site; 🪑). Instead turn right into a remote valley, from where you can enjoy views of distant toy-size farmhouses.

The castles at Montségur (top) and Foix

The next fork, met after a further 5km/3mi, offers three choices: ignore branches to the right (to Trasoulas) and the left; continue ahead, skirting the village of **La Bénague** on your left. Eventually you come to a T-junction with the D29 (60km/37mi) and turn left.

Keep to this road; it becomes the D16. You are now driving along the edge of the **Plateau de Sault**. Eventually you emerge from dense forest. Just past the sign signalling that you are entering **Belesta** (72km/45mi), turn sharp left on the D9 towards FOUGAX ET B./CHATEAU DE MONTSEGUR.

At **Fougax-et-Barrineuf** (77km/48mi) go half-right on the D9 towards 'MONTSEGUR' (*however, a diverson straight ahead on the D5 from to the Gorges de la Frau is called for if you have missed Walk 13; then retrn to the D9 for 'MONTSEGUR'.*)

The D9 is the most attractive route to this famous castle, and the dramatic outline of the stronghold atop a pinnacle mountain soon looms into view ahead. You can't help but wonder how men achieved the 'impossible' task of importing the materials and then building such a magnificent structure. Following the steep-walled road, you appreciate how effective the watchtower high above you must have been against the enemy. The road climbs to **Montségur** village (85km/53mi ✕MWC) and on up to the castle★ (🏛), where the Cathars were besieged for ten months in 1243/44 and eventually massacred.

Some 4km beyond Montségur, ignore the turning left to Mont d'Olmes (it's 14km along the D109 to this ski resort, if you wish to visit it) and continue ahead for 'FOIX 26KM'. At **Montferrier** (91km/56mi) turn right towards LAVELANET but, on approaching Villeneuve d'Olmes, take a left turn for FOIX. This brings you to the D117, where you again turn left. Then, within 1km, take the turning off right — onto the D9a. Heading towards Foix on this higher, more picturesque route through steep fields and rickety barns, you drive below the castle of **Roquefixade** (100km/62mi 🏛).

Continue on this upper road, ignoring all turn-offs to the left. At the junction with the main N20, turn right for **Foix**★ (117km/73mi 🏛🏨▲✕☕⊕MWC). After visiting Foix, where the famous castle towers above the ancient history-rich town, the circle is completed by following the N20 to **Tarascon-sur-Ariège** (135km/84mi).

Car tour 5: DEEP VALLEYS, HIGH PEAKS, PAINTED CAVES

Tarascon-sur-Ariège • Grotte de Niaux • Aulus-les-Bains • Seix • Vallée de Bethmale • St-Girons • St-Lizier • Massat • Bédeilhac • Tarascon-sur-Ariège

168km/104mi; about 5 hours' driving
Walks en route or nearby: 14-16
A circular tour through the deep valleys and over some of the bleak passes that characterise the Ariège; the route visits two of the most important prehistoric painted caves in the world. Note: Tour 5 can be linked with Tour 4 at Tarascon-sur-Ariège.
Picnic suggestions: From **Vicdessos** take the D8 signposted 'Auzat' and continue for 11.3km/7mi to the Etang de Soulcem. Here, in an idyllic setting, close to the **Soulcem River**, are tables and benches (⌐). Walk 14 sets out from here (see pages 82-83). Beyond the **Port de Lers**, the **Etang de Lers** is a small and pretty lake much loved by the local population for boating and picnicking in the summer. It's set in the heart of wild mountain country — *but note: there is no shade at the lake.*

When a French person wants to 'downsize' and 'drop out of the rat race', it's to this part of the Ariège that he or she comes, a region of high mountains, deep valleys, fast-flowing streams and abandoned homes.

At **Tarascon-sur-Ariège** (▲▲ ✕♀; Walks 15 and 16) take the D8, signposted 'VICDESSOS'. You quickly pass through **Niaux** (5km/3mi ▲✕), from where you can visit the **Grotte de Niaux**★ (∩), famous for its prehistoric paintings of bison, horses and ibex (advanced reservation necessary, tel: 05 61 05 10 10). The less well-known Grotte de la Vache (∩) and the Musée Paysan (M) are also well worth visiting.

Just before Vicdessos, the left turn to 'Dolmen Sem' is a short but worthwhile diversion, with spectacular views. In **Vicdessos** (14km/9mi ▲✕) turn right on the D18 towards 'AULUS-LES-BAINS'. *(Or continue on the D8 for Walk 14 or a picnic at the Soulcem dam; allow 23km return.)*

The D18 climbs through wild country to the **Port de Lers** (1517m/4975ft; 26km/16mi 📷). In that desolation you see to the south, the lynx clings to life above the abyss of Pyrenean extinction.

Climb through holiday country of deep woods, walking trails and weekend cabins noticeably

Cave paintings, Grotte de Niaux

Wooden shoes of the Bethmale Valley

unadorned by television aerials, and drop down to the **Etang de Lers**, a much-loved boating and picnicking spot. Ignore the right turn to Massat, and climb to the **Col d'Agnès** (📷). From here you descend some 900m/2950ft, from high mountain country of bleak peaks and basin lakes to the depths of the **Garbet Valley** and to the narrow streets and tall buildings of **Aulus-les-Bains** (40km/25mi ⛺✖). This cool old spa town enjoys one of the most spectacular settings in the Pyrenees.

From Aulus climb steeply out of the valley once more, following signposting to the **Col de la Trappe** (45km/28mi ⛺✖). *(Just 1km from this pass you could make a 10km/6mi round-trip diversion left to Guzet-Neige; △📷 — highly recommended for the views you will enjoy back along your route, down to Aulus in the east and around the increasingly gentler mountains at the edge of the Pyrenees.)* The main tour continues along the narrow **Ustou Valley** on the D8f, at the end of which you turn right, following signposts to 'SEIX'.

Seix (65km/40mi ⛺△✖🍴) is a curious town astride the Salat River and a major centre for canoeing. (If you want to shorten the tour, in Seix follow signs straight on for St-Girons and continue to the D618, there turning right for Tarascon — making a total round trip of 130km/81mi.)

Cross the river and take the D17 which drops down into the **Bethmale Valley** at the **Col de la Core** (1395m/4575ft; 📷). This was once a thriving agricultural community. Having been abandoned and reverted to nature, it is now repopulated with holiday retreats. At **Castillon-en-Couserans** (93km/58mi ⛺🏠△✖🍴) turn right on the D618 to **St-Girons** (106km/66mi ⛺🏠△✖🍴WC), from where you take the main D117 road towards SALIES for a visit to the Roman town of **St-Lizier★** (108km/67mi ✝🍴), with its two cathedrals and surviving fortifications.

From St-Lizier return to St-Girons and then leave this busy town on the D618, signposted 'MASSAT' and 'COL DE PORT'. The road now takes you through the **Gorges de Ribaouto** and the **Gorges de Biert** to **Massat** (138km/86mi ⛺✖🍴). Cross the Arac River and ascend through forest to the **Col de Port** (1250m/4100ft). Then descend to the vast cave★ of **Bédeilhac** (∩) with its paintings and engravings, like Niaux, from the Magdalenian period (more than 10,000 years ago) and to **Tarascon-sur-Ariège** (168km/104mi).

The Noguera Pallaresa, the most powerful river in Spain (Car tour 6)

Car tour 6: PARC NACIONAL D'AIGÜES TORTES

Vielha • Port de la Bonaigua • Espot • Parc Nacional d'Aigües Tortes • Gerri de la Sal • La Pobleta de Bellvei • Pont de Suert • (Caldes de Boí) • Túnel de Vielha • Vielha

215km/133mi; about 6.5 hours' driving

Walks en route or nearby: 17

A huge circuit along the Val d'Aran and into the Parc Nacional d'Aigües Tortes, one of two national parks in the Spanish Pyrenees.

Picnic suggestion: Continue through **Espot** (provisions) following signs for 'Parc Nacional d'Aigües Tortes' and 'Estany (Lake) de Sant Maurici'. Park at the **Prat de Pierró** and picnic on the path to the lake or take a jeep-taxi to the **Estany de Sant Maurici** itself (ample shade). At the nearby Refugi Ernest Mallafré (15min on foot; see Walk 17 and map on page 89) it is possible to obtain refreshments and light meals.

Until the building of the Túnel de Vielha in 1948, the Val d'Aran was one of the most remote valleys in the Spanish Pyrenees, cut off from Spain every winter. The region was chosen as the epicentre for the reintroduction of brown bears from Slovenia who today number around 80. It's also known for its rare butterflies, including the alpine grizzled skipper and the chequered skipper.

Leave **Vielha★** (🛇🏔🏠✕🍽M) by heading eastwards along the valley on the C28, following signs for BAQUEIRA-BERET, and soon passing the right turn for Vielha's ski resort, La Tuca. If you have the time, many of the ancient villages in the valley are well worth visiting — Arties (parador 🏔), Salardú (🛇🏔✕) and Tredos especially. From **Baqueira** (🏔✕) the road ascends steeply from the sadly disfigured valley floor below to the **Port de la Bonaigua** (2072m/6800ft; 22km/14mi 📷), south of which lies the Parc Nacional d'Aigües Tortes. From the pass, the road (now C13) drops steeply to **Esterri d'Aneu** (46km/29mi 🏔✕🍽) at the head of the the **Noguera Pallaresa**, the most powerful river in the country.

After 6km, just south of Guingueta, turn right and drive up to **Espot** (59km/37mi 🏔🏠△✕) and the entrance to the **Parc Nacional d'Aigües Tortes** (the Prat de Pierró; 68km/42mi), from where a jeep-taxi can take you up to the starting point for Walk 17. 'Aigües tortes' means, literally, 'twisted waters' — an irony now that hydro-electric schemes have straightened and controlled them. But away from the dams and pipes, izards still graze and golden eagles soar over the forests of fir, beech and birch shown on pages 88-89.

Return to the main road and continue south along the banks of the wide and powerful Noguera Pallaresa (where the photo opposite was taken) to **Llavorsi** (96km/60mi 🏔🏠✕) and **Gerri de la Sal** (123km/76mi ✕), where you can see the old salt pans★ by the road.

The usual way to continue beyond Gerri is through the gorge, the Estret de Collegats, to La Pobla de Segur and then along the Castelbó River to Senterada. You have that option, but we recommend taking the tiny turning *sharp* right at the entrance to Gerri, where an inconspicuous sign says 'POBLETA DE BELLVEI'; this is magical scenery (📷) all the way to **La**

24 Landscapes of the Pyrenees

Pobleta (140km/87mi), on a road not even shown on some maps.

At La Pobleta, turn left for **Senterada** (144km/89mi) and then right onto the N260. You drive through desolate countryside studded with stone perched villages, up to the **Coll de Perbes** (1530m/5020ft) and then on to **Pont de Suert** (175km/109mi ▲▲♦△✕🍴). Here take the N230 north back towards VIELHA. *(After 1km you have the option of a right turn to Caldes de Boí, a resort on the western fringe of the national park; allow 44km/27mi return).* The main tour continues to the **Túnel de Vielha** and back to **Vielha** itself (215km/133mi).

The Riu Escrita at Espot, en route to the entrance to the Parc Nacional d'Aigües Tortes

Car tour 7: 'GROTTES' AND GARGOYLES

Bagnères-de-Bigorre • Abbaye d'Escaladieu • Château de Mauvezin • (Esparros) • Grottes de Gargas • St-Bertrand-de-Comminges • Luchon • Col de Peyresourde • Arreau • Col d'Aspin • Bagnères-de-Bigorre

162km/100mi; about 5 hours' driving
Walks en route or nearby: 18, 19
Good surfaced roads are used throughout this tour.
Picnic suggestion: The **Col d'Aspin**, above **Arreau**, is one of the 'high spots' of this long car tour and commands breathtaking views in all directions (note the landmark of the radio-masted Pic du Midi de Bigorre to the west). *NB: The pass can be quite exposed, and there is no shade.*

To see or not to see, that will be your question, for this circuit passes the Abbey of Escaladieu, the Château de Mauvezin, the prehistoric Grottes de Gargas with their weird 'deformed-hand' imprints, the magnificent St-Bertrand-de-Comminges, the Grotte de Médous — and many beauty spots, from the Baronnies foothills to the heights of the Col d'Aspin.

Leave **Bagnères-de-Bigorrre** (🏨♨️⛺️✕🅿️WC) on the D938, following signs for TOULOUSE and CAPVERN. At **Le Hailla** (7km/4.5mi) ignore the left fork to Tournay (D20) and continue on the D938 to the ancient abbey★ (⛪) of **Escaladieu** (13km/8mi) and then on to the **Château de Mauvezin**★ (🏨📷) on the hilltop above.

From the château descend once more towards Escaladieu and, shortly before you return to the abbey, turn left by the Auberge l'Arros on the D14 (signposted 'BONNEMAZON'). Just before Bourg-de-Bigorre, cross the Arros River and continue following the D14, ignoring turn-offs and keeping the river on your right at first. Climb to **Espèche** and then past **Lomne**, to the junction with the D26 (24km/15mi). From here a right turn would take you into the village of **Esparros** 1km away (♨️; Walk 18). But the main tour turns left for the **Col de Coupe** (720m/2360ft; 26km/16mi 📷) with its views back to the velvety green and verdant hillsides.

At the junction with the main D929 turn right in the direction of HÈCHES and, very soon afterwards, left (just beyond a petrol station); follow the signs to 'BAZUS-NESTE' on the D78. Soon coming to a junction, turn right for 'ST-ARROMAN'. At the next junction, go left on the D26 and through **St-Arroman** (36km/23mi). Shortly afterwards fork right (signposted 'NESTIER'), still on the D26. Ignoring all turnings off the road, continue straight on through **Nestier**, to the pleasant village of **Aventignan**, just beyond which you turn right to the **Grottes de Gargas**★ (48km/30mi 🏨∩✕WC).

Regaining the main road from the caves, turn right. **St-Bertrand-de-Comminges**★, one of the most important religious monuments in the Pyrenees (56km/35mi ⛪🍴✕WC) is soon visible on a hilltop. The tour continues via **Valcabrère** (from where you can make a short diversion to the nearby 11th-century church of St-Just★ (⛪📷) and enjoy splendid views back to St-Bertrand.

Some 2km beyond Valcabrère head south on the N125 and then the D125 for **Luchon**★ (also known as Bagnères-de-Luchon; 89km/55mi 🏨♨️⛺️✕🅿️MWC). (To approach Walk 19, take the D125 south for

Arrau

'HOSPICE DE FRANCE'.) Leave Luchon westwards on the D618 (signposted 'COL DE PEYRESOURDE'), having first made sure that the signs are green, confirmation that the pass is open. The road climbs steeply to the precipitous village of **St-Aventin** (93km/58mi ✝) and on through **Garin** (96km/60mi ⛺✖) to the **Col de Peyresourde** (1569m/5145ft; 108km/67mi 📷).

From the col, descend on the D618 through magnificent scenery, ignoring side-turnings, to **Arreau** (125km/78mi ⛺♠✖🚻WC), with its attractive half-timbered buildings and covered market. Cross a bridge by the Office du Tourism, turn right onto the D929 (signposted 'COL

St-Bertrand-de-Comminges

D'ASPIN') and then almost immediately left onto the D918 (still signposted for the col). The steep 12km climb passes the lovely village of **Aspin-Aure**, a forestry community said to be one of the richest in the *département*. At the **Col d'Aspin** (📷 1489m/4885ft; 137km/85mi) — a lovely, if exposed, picnic spot — stop to admire the views south to the frontier peaks and ahead to the Pic du Midi de Bigorre with its peak-top observatory.

The tour now makes its final descent through forest to the wide **Plateau de Payolle** and its pleasant lake (143km/89mi ⛺✖) and **Ste-Marie-de-Campan** (150km/93mi ✝⛺✖🚻WC), where you turn right on the D935. At **Campan** (✝⛺△✖) the 17th-century church and the **Grotte de Médous★** (∩), with their dramatic limestone formations, are the final attractions en route, before you return to **Bagnères-de-Bigorre** (162km/100mi).

Car tour 8: MARVELS AND MIRACLES

Lourdes • Bagnères-de-Bigorre • Ste-Marie-de-Campan • La Mongie • Col du Tourmalet • Barèges • Luz-St-Sauveur • Cirque de Gavarnie • (Beaucens or Cauterets) • Argelès-Gazost • Agos Vidalos • Lourdes

148km/92mi; about 4 hours' driving
Walks en route and nearby: 20-23
A comfortable circular route on good surfaced roads, starting at the famous pilgrimage town of Lourdes and including the most visited spectacle of the whole Pyrenees, the Cirque de Gavarnie.
Picnic suggestion: After parking in **Gavarnie** (WC, refreshments) follow the crowds towards the splendour of the *cirque,* passing several tables and benches set in dense woods (🪑). However, for maximum viewing pleasure, continue to walk for a further 10 minutes to the **Plateau de la Prade**. There you will find a secluded spot amongst shady bushes by the stream — the young Gave du Gavarnie, which you have followed through the long valley. An alternative would be to hire the services of a pony to carry you and your picnic to the base of the *cirque.* See the map on page 95 (Walk 20).

Beginning and ending at the world-famous pilgrimage centre of Lourdes, this tour visits perhaps the best-known landscape in the Pyrenees — the fabulous Cirque de Gavarnie. You might also like to take the time to explore Cauterets, a mountain resort much loved by the Empress Eugénie.

From the large roundabout at the southern edge of **Lourdes★** (✝🏨🏕🍴⛽WC), head south on the D921b for GER, but after 1.6km (just before a bridge on the right over the Gave du Pau), turn left on the D13 for GER. After 0.45km, at a T-junction, turn left (D26; signposted 'ST-CREAC') and continue through a gentle green landscape

Glacier d'Ossoue, west of Gavarnie (Walk 21)

with its southern backdrop of high mountains to **Pouzac** (22km/14mi). Turn right onto the D935, quickly arriving at **Bagnères-de-Bigorre** (26km/16mi ▲▲♦△✕➡WC).

Take the D935 south out of Bagnères, following clear overhead signs for 'LES COLS' and, after 2km, pass the wrought-iron entrance to the **Grotte de Médous**★ (∩). Pass through **Campan** (32km/20mi ✝▲ △✕) and **Ste-Marie-de-Campan** (38km/24mi ✝▲✕WC). in Ste-Marie, turn right onto the D918 westwards, following signs for 'COL DU TOURMALET' and 'LA MONGIE'.

From **La Mongie** (54km/34mi ▲▲♦✕) climb over towards the neighbouring resort of Barèges (together these form the biggest ski domain in the Pyrenees) via the **Col du Tourmalet** (2115m/6940ft; 58km/36mi ✕☞WC). *(From this pass you could drive almost to the summit of the Pic du Midi de Bigorre (2872m/9420ft) on a toll-road; allow 14km/9mi return.)*

The descent from the col is a spectacle of hairpin bends and high mountain scenery all the way to **Barèges** (69km/43mi ▲▲♦✕➡WC) and **Luz-St-Sauveur**★ (76km/49mi ✝▲▲♦△✕➡WC). Turn sharp left in the village centre onto the D921, signposted 'GAVARNIE' and, at the bridge, bear left, keeping the **Gave de Gavarnie** to the right and the elegant spa buildings of St-Sauveur on the opposite bank.

As you climb beyond **Gèdre** (88km/55mi ▲▲♦✕), past the turning left to the Cirque de Troumouse (less visited than Gavarnie), the incredible **Cirque de Gavarnie**★ begins to emerge, and you enjoy the view shown in the photo on pages 96-97. The famous 'gateway' in its rim, the Brèche de Roland (Walk 22; photo on pages 100-101), is clearly visible.

Gavarnie★ (96km/60mi ✝▲ ♦✕☞⌂WC; Walks 20-22) is a tourist village of hotels, restaurants and souvenir shops, but it is nevertheless the soul of the French Pyrenees and for over a century the starting-out point for the great exploits of many famous mountaineers. A short walk to the Plateau de la Prade — perhaps with a picnic — is highly recommended.

Return to Luz-St-Sauveur (116km/72mi) and, at the square, turn left following signs for ARGELÈS-GAZOST and LOURDES (still the D921). After about 2km, turn right off the main road to **Saligos** and **Chèze**, before this minor road merges with the D921 for LOURDES again; it runs through gorge-type scenery of steep cliffs, beside a wide river. Continue to **Soulom** (127km/ 79mi). *(Here you could take a detour to the right, to BEAUCENS, to see the birds of prey at the 'Donjon des Aigles'; allow 8km/5mi return.)* The next village en route is **Pierrefitte-Nestalas**. *(A detour to the left leads to CAUTERETS and the setting for Walk 23; 21km/13mi return.)*

The main tour follows the D921 to **Argelès-Gazost** (136km/84mi ▲▲♦△✕➡), then the D921B to **Agos Vidalos** (141km/87mi ▲✕), a village dominated on the left by the *'montagne enchantée',* the Pic de Pibeste. The mountain's strange Mediterranean micro-climate supports the mouflon (rare wild sheep) and some plant species that are equally rare in the Pyrenees. (For information on the Pic de Pibeste, stop at the Maison de la Réserve in Agos Vidalos, tel: 05 62 97 14 55.) Continue on the main road back to **Lourdes** (148km/92mi).

Car tour 9: GRAND CANYONS TOUR

Torla-Ordesa • Sarvisé • Fanlo • Buerba • Escalona • Hospital de Tella • Revilla • Bielsa • Valle de Pineta • Bielsa • Escalona • Desfiladero de Vellos (Añisclo Canyon) • Torla-Ordesa

215km/133mi; about 5 hours' driving
Walks en route and nearby: 24-26
A demanding drive across remote mountain wilderness and with optional visits to some of the world's most spectacular and unspoilt canyons.
Picnic suggestion: From **Torla-Ordesa** head north and after 3km take the track to the left through the Garganta de los Navarros that leads to Camping de Bujaruelo and then Bujaruelo. Here, along the banks of the **Ara River**, you'll find few people but possibly marmots and izards.

V isiting this incredibly beautiful region, you may wonder why it is not better known internationally. The main canyon, the Ordesa, with its kilometre-high walls, rivals America's famous Grand Canyon for spectacle.

Torla-Ordesa (🏠🏕⛺🍴) is the gateway to the fabulous **Parque Nacional de Ordesa y Monte Perdido★** and the obvious place to stay in this region. The main canyon, with its 1000m/3300ft walls, demands at the very least a day of its own (see Walk 26). For our drive we will head south and east to take in some of the other spectacles of the area.

Head south from Torla-Ordesa on the A135, then N260a, watching out for the breathtaking acrobatics of beautiful red kites, often seen here. Continue through **Broto** (20km/12.5mi 🏠🏕🍴☕) and, at **Sarvisé** (23km/14mi), turn left on the HU631 towards FANLO.

This little road rises along the **Chate River** to almost eerie views of the desolate plateaux that top the Ordesa Canyon. **Fanlo** (32km/20mi 📷), a once-deserted village now renovated for holiday homes, is worth a stop for the views and the park information office.

The road now bypasses Nerin (📷), to wind along the deepening gorge of the **Aso River**. At the next junction (39km/24mi) turn right for **Buerba**. The road climbs up to a viewpoint from which you can see along the exquisite **Añisclo Canyon** (Walk 25), then wriggles its way spectacularly high above the **Vellos (Bellos) River** to **Puyarruego** (55km/34mi). Later we will be returning along the Vellos River, but for now turn right, and on reaching the main road (A138) at **Escalona**, turn left towards BIELSA.

On the far side of **Hospital de Tella** (66km/41mi), turn left,

Torla, gateway to the Ordesa and Monte Perdido National Park

following signs for TELLA. After some 2km the road divides. Try first the upper, right-hand route, leading to **Tella** (69km/43mi ✛) with its Hermitage of Juanipablo and the Virgen de la Peña. Then return and take the other, lower, road, on a shelf over the stunning **Yaga Canyon**. At **Revilla** (75km/47mi 📷) there is an easy 2h return walk to a look-out point ('*mirador*') signposted from the village.

Return to the A138 and continue into **Bielsa**★ (92km/57mi ▲✕🍽M), a border-style shopping town. Leaving the square, follow signs for 'VALLE DE PINETA' and 'PARADOR'.

You come to the splendid **Pineta Valley**, shown on pages 106-107 (Walk 24). The *parador* (115km/71mi ▲) stands at the end of the road, at the foot of the **Circo de Pineta** — a rock amphitheatre comparable to the famous French *cirques* of Gavarnie and Troumouse.

Return to **Escalona**, where you have a choice. We recommend you turn right for **Puyarruego** and then follow the road through the **Desfiladero de Vellos**, past the entrance to the Añisclo Canyon (Walk 25). The *desfiladero* is an experience you should not miss, the gorge so narrow in places that a one-way system (east to west) is in operation.

Once through the *desfiladero*, retrace your route to **Torla-Ordesa** (215km/133mi). (However, if you are in a hurry to get back to Torla-Ordesa, it is actually quicker to continue on straight roads — the A138 to Ainsa and then the N260 for Boltaña and Torla-Ordesa, saving almost 20km.)

Monte Perdido (Walk 26), the third-highest mountain in the Pyrenees and the highest limestone massif in Europe

Car tour 10: THE VALLEY OF THE BEAR

Jaca • Puente la Reina de Jaca • (Hecho • Selva de Oza) • Ansó • Col Belagua • Arette-Pierre-St-Martin • Aspe Valley • (Lescun) • Candanchú • Jaca

158km/98mi; a little under 5 hours' driving.
Walk nearby: 27
This tour makes the most of good sealed roads, even in the high mountains.
Picnic suggestion: At the 42km-point, instead of turning off just before **Hecho** for Ansó, continue straight down the fabulously scenic Hecho Valley for 12km/7mi, until you reach the **Selva** (forest) **de Oza**, a popular recreational area with full camping and walking facilities (⌐WC; refreshments).

This is an area so magnificently wild that it was home to the last Pyrenean brown bear, Camille, who died in 2010. Today, thanks to reintroductions from Slovenia, there are at least 80 brown bears in the Pyrenees (see Car tour 6). You can see two of them in the Parc'Ours in the Aspe Valley,

Leave **Jaca** (✝🏔🏠△✕🚏WC) with its extravagant buildings, busy shopping streets, and almost ever-circling vultures, by taking the N240 — the main road to Pamplona. Almost immediately you come upon the windswept plains of the **Río Aragón**. After 10km/6mi pass signs to Santa Cruz de la Serós and the famous mountain monastery of San Juán de la Peña (✝). In 19km/12mi you cross the bridge at **Puente la Reina** (🏔✕🚏) by turning right, following signs to 'HECHO' on the A176, a well-surfaced road running through open pastureland towards the forests and mountains ahead.

About 1km before Hecho (42km/26mi 🏔🏠✕) take a left turn to ANSO* (still the A176). The easy and attractive road undulates for 10km to **Ansó** (52km/32mi ✝🏔✕), with its cobbled streets and wooden balconies. Leave Ansó for ZURIZA, keeping the river on your left and enjoying more spectacular scenery as the journey progresses through woods of Scots pine, fir and oak.

As the valley narrows, so the mountains become higher and the population, so it is said, becomes increasingly idiosyncratic, often wearing traditional dress (the nearest

---

*But to see more of this beautiful valley, follow the road through **Hecho** and go on to **Siresa** with its 9th-century monastery (✝). Continuing through gorge-like scenery, you come to the popular leisure complex of the **Selva de Oza**. This lovely forest *(selva)* is a very pleasant place to picnic.

31

Lescun — an optional detour of 11km return, and the starting point for Walk 27, illustrated on pages 114-117

to 'native' dress we once saw was a farmer with an animal skin thrown over his shoulders for warmth).

As you approach the cross-country skiing resort of **Zuriza** (66km/41mi ⛺▲✕), the gorge-like landscape opens out into a wide bowl. Just before the village, take the NA2000 to the left, climbing steeply through open hillside (📷) to a pass, where you leave Aragón and enter Navarra, before dropping down towards ISABA. At 78km/48mi come to a T-junction with the NA137 where, instead of going into Isaba to the left, you turn right for the FRENCH FRONTIER via the **Belagua Pass** (📷).

Cross the border (102km/63mi) and enter a weird landscape of karst (limestone), eerily eroded above and penetrated below you by a labyrinth of tunnels and caves. (The caverns of Pierre-St-Martin, discovered in 1952, are amongst the deepest in the world — the entrance, just on the Spanish side, bears a memorial to speleologist Marcel Loubens who died in them.)

Leave the skiing resort of **Arette-Pierre-St-Martin** (⛺▲✕) on the D132 (signposted 'ARETTE') and, after 6km (108km/67mi), take the right-hand fork (D441) to the **Col de Bouésou** (114km/71mi). Travelling through forests of huge beech trees, you come upon the pretty stone-built village of **Lées-Athas** (122km/76mi). You enter the village on the D441 to **Athas**; partway along, be sure to turn right on the D237 to **Lees**, to reach the junction with the N134 (the main **Vallée d'Aspe** road)

Turn left towards the Spanish border. *(After 2km a turning right leads to the picturesque village of Lescun; this optional detour of 11km/7mi would take you to the setting shown above and Walk 27. Some 5km further on is the turn-off right to Borce, where you'll find the Parc'Ours signposted.)*

Beyond **Urdos** (127km/79mi ⛺✕) the road climbs through the Parc National des Pyrénées to the frontier, below which is the modern ski resort of **Candanchú** (⛺✕) and, 9km below it, the **Canfranc** railway terminus (135km/84mi).

From here follow the valley back to **Jaca** (158km/98mi).

Car tour 11: LIMESTONE AND LEGENDS

St-Jean-Pied-de-Port • Col Burdincurutcheta • Col d'Orgambidesca • Larrau • Ste-Engrâce • Arette-Pierre-St-Martin • Isaba • Ochagavía • (Pamplona) • Burguete • Roncesvalles • Puerto de Ibañeta • St-Jean-Pied-de-Port

189km/117mi; about 5 hours' driving.
Walks en route and nearby: 28, 29
A long day, first visiting the gorges and startling limestone landscape of the Pic d'Anie region, then with the option of spending time in Pamplona — before returning to France via the Ibañeta Pass, scene of the legendary 'Chanson de Roland'.
Picnic suggestion: From **Roncesvalles**, continue up the hill, towards the border. After five minutes you emerge on a virtually treeless hilltop, the **Puerto de Ibañeta** (map pages 120-121), where you can park, walk and see the memorial to Roland shown on page 118. *NB: There is no shade at this pass.*

Enjoy a change from the high peaks of the central Pyrenees. This tour takes you through rolling green countryside, liberally sprinkled with large white houses and well-tended farms. Luckily the roads are much easier to negotiate than the Basque language ...

Leave the attractive old market town of **St-Jean-Pied-de-Port** (🏠▲△✖ ♨WC; best access to Walk 28) eastwards on the D933 in the direction of **St-Jean-le-Vieux** (4.5km/3mi), and there leave the main road by turning right onto the D18, following signs for *'STATION DE SKI D'IRATY.'*

Beyond **Lecumberry** and **Mendive** (11km/7mi), the road climbs steeply through scenery at first reminiscent of the English Lake District, but soon revealing its more awesome scale at the **Col Burdincurutcheta** (1135m/ 3725ft; 24km/15mi 📷), from where you have views towards the huge Iraty Forest ahead. Descend to a small dried-up lake, only to climb again by turning left on the D19 for Larrau. You pass **Camping Iraty** (△) and the **Col d'Orgambidesca** (1319m/4325ft; 33.5km/21mi 📷), one of the most important bird migration routes in Europe and the scene of bitter confrontation between conservationists and hunters.

Descend through a series of steep hairpin bends to **Larrau** (46.5km/29mi 🏠▲✖), from where we head northeast on the D26 which runs alongside the Gave (river) de Larrau to **Laugibar** (▲✖), where you could see the Crevasses d'Holzarté.

Beyond Laugibar turn right (55km/34mi) on the D113. Via the **Gorges de Kakouetta** and **Ste-Engrâce** (66km/41mi ✝) climb steeply up to the junction with the D132 and here turn right into the ski station of **Arette-Pierre-St-Martin** (76km/47mi 🏠▲✖). You're amidst the spikes and spines, faults and flues of some of the most outrageous limestone scenery anywhere in the world.

Continue on the D132, the border road. Just across the frontier (now the NA137) lies the now-barred entrance to the **Gouffre Pierre-St-Martin**, where speleologist Marcel Loubens died during the early exploration of what was then the deepest known cavern in the world. Your descent, above ground, to **Isaba** (103km/64mi

33

34 Landscapes of the Pyrenees

⛰🏠✕🍴) is breathtakingly beautiful. (Tour 10 follows this section, but in the reverse direction.)

At Isaba continue on the NA140 to **Uztárroz** and **Ochagavía**, driving through a densely-forested landscape. Basque-style architecture comes into view more frequently: the huge square village and farm houses are spotlessly white-washed and roofed in slate or tiles.

At **Escároz** (124km/77mi) cross the Salazar River and turn right (signposted *'BURGUETE'*). On reaching the N135 some 30km/19mi further on, decide whether to turn right with the main tour into **Burguete** (156km/97mi ⛰✕) or left for a 90km/56mi round trip detour to Pamplona. Burguete was made famous by Hemingway in *The Sun Also Rises*.

From Burguete the road back to St-Jean-Pied-de-Port passes **Roncesvalles** (159km/99mi ✝⛰✕M; Walk 29), with its unmistakable collegiate buildings and fascinating history. A little further along it climbs to the **Ibañeta Pass** (1062m/3485ft 📷), the most likely site for the massacre of Charlemagne's rearguard by the Basques in revenge for the sacking of Pamplona. The battle's inaccurate celebration in the *Chanson de Roland* is the explanation for the memorial at the pass (photo on page 118), which is also on the famous pilgrims' route to Santiago de Compostela. The pass is a good place to picnic on fine days.

The road now descends to **Valcarlos** and then a further 3km to the frontier at **Arnéguy**, for the final sprint back to **St-Jean-Pied-de-Port** (189km/117mi).

Landscape in the Basque country (Car tour 12)

Car tour 12: INTO THE BASQUE COUNTRY

San Sebastián • Hernani • Goizueta • Doneztebe-Santesteban • Elizondo • St-Etienne-de-Baïgorry • Bidarray • Pas de Roland • Ainhoa • La Rhune • St-Jean-de-Luz

205km/127mi; about 4 hours' driving; from the AP1 motorway at San Sebastián take the A15 and then the GI3410 towards Goizueta.
Walks en route and nearby: 30-34
A full day out, beginning and ending on the coastal motorway for easy access, and visiting wild country on both sides of the border.
Picnic suggestion: Continue on the D4 from **Dantxarinea**, keeping on the French side of the border, and crossing the River Nivelle by the **Pont du Diable**. You drive through an ancient oak forest, with good parking and picnicking possibilities. You could also stretch your legs by following the GR10 to the east or west.

Although the Basque country borders the densely-populated Atlantic coastal resorts, this tour takes you quickly and easily into a region most tourists never visit. Driving is relaxing, signposting good; you should have time to take the train up the mountain landmark of La Rhune ... or, better still, climb up!

From the Spanish coastal AP1 motorway near **San Sebastián★** (✝🏠▲♦✕♇⊕MWC) take the A15 and then the GI3410 signposted 'GOIZUETA' and 'FAGOLLAGA'. The ugly industrial development begins to be left behind at **Ereñotzu** and the road (soon the NA4150) climbs steeply through densely-forested mountains to **Goizueta** (35km/22mi). When you reach the NA170 (50km/31mi ▲), turn left, following signposts for 'DONEZTEBE-SANTESTEBAN'.

The scenery is more pastoral now, the great forests felled for agriculture, much as on the French side of the border. Descend along the **Ezkurra River**, at one stage through a gorge, to **Doneztebe-Santesteban** (74km/46mi ▲✕), where you join the N121A towards PAMPLONA (right). After 4km, turn left on the N121B towards FRANCIA and ELIZONDO. After crossing the Bastan River, turn right at a roundabout for ARRAIOZ/IRURITA, then go left immediately for IRURITA (NA8307). In **Irurita** (♇ nearby) bear left to **Elizondo** (♇), beyond which you rejoin the N121B at another roundabout and turn right. In **Ordoki** (94km/58mi) turn right on the NA2600 for Errazu, thereafter climbing steeply towards the

35

St-Jean-de-Luz

COL D'ISPEGUY and the frontier.

The road cuts through wild country of moor and rock to intersect the famous Basque landmark of the **Iparla Ridge** (Walk 30; photo on page 123) at the **Col d'Ispéguy** (📷). From the quiet frontier post, with its one or two shops, descend to **St-Etienne-de-Baïgorry** (112km/70mi ▲▲♦✕☎) on the D949.

Turn left along the D948, cross the Nive River, and turn left again onto the D918 for **Bidarray** (126km/78mi ▲▲✕; photo on page 124). (*Alternatively, some 3km beyond St-Etienne-de-Baïgorry, you could make a left turn down a tiny tarmac track signposted 'La Bastide' and follow green arrows to Bidarray, with fine views of the Iparla Ridge.*)

From Bidarray follow the main road for 12km to **Itxassou** (▲▲♦✕), turn left into the village, and from there follow signs to the **Pas de Roland★**, a curious rock formation in a gorge. According to legend, the gap was created by Roland's horse (see notes with Walks 28 and 29).

Take the D249 out of Itxassou to **Espelette** (▲▲♦✕), just after which you turn left towards AINHOA on the D20. After 1km (☎ just before) turn left again into **Ainhoa** (150km/93mi ▲▲✕). From here go on to the old border post at **Dantxarinea** and there turn right (north) along the **Nivelle River** (D4). Still in France, you travel through an ancient oak wood (there are pleasant riverside picnic spots where the road crosses the Nivelle via the **Pont du Diable**).

When you reach a T-junction, turn left (D4) to **Sare** and from there continue on the D4 for ASCAIN. Some 3km along you have the option of taking the rack railway to the top of **La Rhune★** (Larroun; 900m/2950ft; photo on page 125), the highest peak in the region, with views inland and all along the coast. Legend has it that witches used to gather on the summit.

Once in **Ascain**, follow signposting to nearby ST-JEAN-DE-LUZ. (*From Ascain you can also make a detour southwest to the Col d'Ibardin, a 'mini-Andorra' — do a bit of shopping or stretch your legs in the settings shown on pages 128-130: bear left on the D4 to Herboure, and from there head south on the D404. For a shorter version of Walk 32 see 'How to get there' on page 129; for Walk 33 see page 131.*)*

Finally arriving at **St-Jean-de-Luz★** (176km/109mi ▲▲♦△✕☎WC), you can regain the motorway. The return to your starting point, on the Spanish side of the border, brings the total distance for the circular tour to 205km/127mi. To get to Walks 31 and 32,* leave the motorway immediately after crossing the Bidasoa River, which is the frontier, following signs for Hendaye, and then turn left under the motorway onto the D258, into Biriatou (1.4km from the motorway exit). If you're making for the Peñas de Aia* (Walk 34; photo on pages 132-133), take the D810 towards Irún.

*For an overview of all the walks in this area, see the map on pages 126-127.)

Country code for walkers and motorists

The experienced rambler is used to following a 'country code', but the tourist out for a lark may unwittingly cause damage, harm animals, and even endanger his own life. Do heed this advice:

- **Do not light fires.** Use camping stoves. Stub out cigarettes with care.
- **Do not frighten animals.** By making loud noises or trying to touch or photograph them, you may cause them to run in fear and be hurt.
- **Walk quietly** through all farms, hamlets and villages, **leaving gates just as you found them**. Gates do have a purpose, usually they keep animals in — or out of — an area.
- **Protect all wild and cultivated plants**. Don't try to pick wild flowers or uproot saplings. Obviously fruit and crops are someone's private property and should not be touched. Never raid anyone's wood pile.
- **Take all your litter away with you**.
- **Stay on the path** wherever it exists, to minimise damage to surrounding vegetation. Don't take short cuts on zigzag paths; this hastens ground erosion.
- **Respect local bye-laws**, especially with reference to camping *'sauvage'*. Always choose an unobtrusive site.
- **Keep well away from streams** when attending to 'calls of nature'. Do not use detergents for washing or washing-up.
- **Support** the small local shopkeepers and artisans whenever you can.
- *Special warning:* Afternoon thunderstorms are common in the Pyrenees (see 'Weather' on page 38). It can be a very frightening experience to be on an exposed mountain area when they strike. Take heed of weather reports and do ask local advice before starting off on exposed mountain walks. In thundery weather, it is always a good idea to set off very early in the day, so that you will be down off the mountainous areas by early afternoon.

Red kite. While you are in the Cauterets area (Car tour 8), you can see birds of prey, including griffon vultures and lammergeiers at the Donjon des Aigles in nearby Beaucens.

Walking

There are well over 400 kilometres (250 miles) of walks in this guide, the equivalent of a coast-to-coast traverse — one of the 'classics' for all serious walkers. But you don't have to be an expert walker for any of hikes we describe. None requires special skills (under summer conditions) and, if you are not very fit, simply turn back when you feel like it (there are short walk suggestions with most of the itineraries). Experienced and fit walkers will nevertheless find much to enjoy, for we have included some of the wildest scenery in the Pyrenees, walked pilgrim routes and World War 2 escape routes, climbed to summits (like Canigou), enjoyed the habitat of marmots, vultures and izards (the Pyrenean chamois), and not neglected the great and the famous (like the Brèche de Roland).

Grading, waymarking, maps, GPS

We've tried to give you a quick overview of each walk's **grade** in the Contents. But we've only had space to show the *lowest* grade of a *main* walk: for full details, including easier versions, see the walk itself. Here is a brief overview of the three gradings:

- **Easy:** good surface; limited ascent (no more than about 600m/2000ft); no technical skill or special equipment required; may still be long.
- **Moderate:** changeable surface; usually a steep ascent/descent; the walk may be very long.
- **Difficult:** may involve any or all of the following: scrambling over difficult surfaces; prolonged exposure, steep ascents/descents; poor signposting. Suitable walking equipment required.

Any of the above grades may be followed by:

- danger of vertigo: you must be sure-footed, with a head for heights

Waymarking in the Pyrenees is mostly *(but not always)* of European standard, as described below:

- **long-distance footpaths**, or **'GR' routes**: in Spanish 'Grandes Recorridos', in French 'Grandes Randonnées', indicated by *red and white* waymarks;
- **day trails** which may be prefaced by **'PR'** (for 'Pequeños Recorridos' or 'Petites Randonnées') and indicated by *yellow and white* waymarks
- **local walks**, prefaced **'SL'** (for 'Senderos Locales' or 'Sentiers Locals') and indicated by *green and white* waymarks.

But other walks may have idiosyncratic local waymarking colours or use special symbols (like the shell incorporated into Camino de Santiago signposts). Then there will be trails not signed or waymarked in any way and for which you will have to rely entirely upon the descriptions and maps in this book.

For all routes, horizontal stripes (=) indicate 'continue this way', angled (∠) or right-angled stripes show a change of direction; an 'X' (✗) means 'wrong way'.

The **maps** in this book should be sufficient for all the walks you plan — enough for four weeks' walking every day. And you will save a great deal of money, since you would need almost twenty large-scale maps to cover walking routes throughout the range. Our maps are based on Openstreet mapping (see page 2), heavily annotated from our notes and GPS work. We have found them to be *very* accurate on the ground. It is a pity that we have to reproduce them at only 1:50,000 to keep the book to a reasonable size; some walkers buy both the paperback *and* download our pdf files so that they can enlarge the maps — or they can be enlarged on a colour photocopier.

Should you wish to buy some good large-scale area maps, showing all the GR routes and overnight hostels, Rando Editions (together with various partners) publishes maps for the entire Pyrenees at a scale of 1:50,000, providing sufficient detail for most purposes. In many cases these maps cover both the **French** and **Spanish** sides of the range on a single sheet. However, if you require more detail, there are 1:25,000 IGN maps for the **French Pyrenees** and **Andorra** (the 'TOP 25' Series). Some parts of the **Spanish Pyrenees** are also covered by Editorial Alpina and the Institut Cartgràfic de Catalunya.

Free **GPS track** downloads are available for all our walks: see the Pyrenees page on the Sunflower website. Please bear in mind, however, that GPS readings should *never* be relied upon as your sole reference point, as conditions can change overnight. *But even if you don't use GPS,* our maps are now so accurate that you can easily compare them with Google Maps on your smartphone and pinpoint your exact position. And it's great fun opening our GPX files in Google Earth to preview the walks in advance!

Safety and guides

Safe walking in the mountains is a matter of judgement, just like driving a car or crossing a road. And that judgement cannot easily be taught in books; it has to be acquired, preferably by going with other experienced walkers. If you are a novice, begin with some of the lower, shorter walks, take it easy, and build from there. Much is made of the dangers of walking alone, but also it can be dangerous to be the slowest and weakest member of an aggressive party. (It also causes no end of worry to set off in a group and then split up with the intention of somehow meeting again later.) *Judgement!* In season, on popular routes, the solo walker in trouble will find help near at hand; out of season, or in more remote parts, self-help (and that implies two or more people) is the only solution.

Should you wish to hire a **guide** for any walks in the region, enquire at the nearest tourist information office.

Weather

Walking in the mountains is very dependent on weather conditions. A walk that can be completed quickly in the early cool of a summer morning can become an endurance test in the midday heat — or positively dangerous in the afternoon, when ferocious thunderstorms frequently erupt. A walk that demands no particular skill in late summer can require special snow and ice equipment in spring — even as late as June — and may be almost impassable with the onset of autumn storms. In the high mountains of the Pyrenees there can be snow at any time of year, even in August. *Always* take local advice before setting off on walks over 2000m in summer and above 1000m in winter.

Naturally there is variation in climate. In general, the eastern and Spanish Pyrenees (excepting the Basque country) enjoy a drier Mediterranean-type climate. If the weather is bad in France, it may be better in Spain. But you don't necessarily have to go south for sun: climbing may also work, for at 1800m you may be above the clouds.

AVERAGE TEMPERATURES

Degrees Centigrade

	Mar-Apr	May-June	Jul-Aug	Sept-Oct
Midi-Pyrénées	7.8	17.5	20.8	18.3
Pyrénées-Roussillon	16.3	23.1	28.1	22.9
Basque Country	14.9	20.1	24.0	21.1

Transport

For non-circular itineraries we recommend getting the transport problems out of the way *before* you start the walk; if you have a car, leave it at the **destination** and take public transport to the **start** of the walk. Then you won't have to worry about missing buses or trains at the end of the day.

Clothing and equipment

Style of walking is a personal matter, and the novice will have to find his or her own. There is a minimum of equipment for safety on certain walks in this book, but remember that a law of diminishing returns is in operation. The more you carry the slower you go, so the more you need to carry. As far as clothing is concerned, flexibility is paramount; it is vital to be able to strip down to shorts and T-shirt when the going gets hot and then cover up by stages as evening approaches or as you climb (reckon on the temperature falling 1 degree Centigrade for every 100m to 200m of ascent — say every 500ft).

Time of year/weather is the most important factor to consider, when you're planning what equipment to take. The Brèche de Roland, for example (one of the most famous goals for walkers in the Pyrenees), normally requires no special equipment in August but may call for crampons, ice-axe and rope in the winter. In particular, beware of old snow in late spring and early summer on steep slopes. It may look like fun but can be rotten and unable to support your weight. Even crampons and ice-axes may then be of no use.

Total distance, metres of ascent, availability of supplies, and the existence of 'escape routes' (quick ways back to safety) are other factors. Below we give a checklist of equipment you *might* take: you will have to use your own judgement about what is right for you.

Backpack or small rucksack
Compass, GPS
Stove and fuel, Matches
Sunhat
Sunglasses, suncream
Warm hat
Gloves
Torch or headlamp
Gaiters
Waterproof trousers
Waterproofs
Survival bag (in case of accident)
Area map (1:25,000 or 1:50,000)
First aid kit
Food and water
Sleeping bag or sheet (for refuges)
Crampons, Rope
Bivvi sac or lightweight tent (for sleeping out)
Ice axe
Warm undergarments
Fleece
Mobile/smartphone (the **emergency number is 112**)
Windcheater

Food and water

Some of the itineraries described visit mountain refuges where meals can be obtained (*always telephone in advance to confirm that they are open, even in summer*), but usually you will have to carry food with you. The correct amount of food for you is something that can only be discovered by experience, but remember that food is fuel and, when you are running down at the end of the day, a fast-energy food can give you a terrific boost.

Water is even more vital, but we often find it impossible to carry enough. In the high mountains of the Pyrenees it is safe to drink from streams, provided there is no habitation above you (mountain villages invariably flush toilets directly into streams). Check your map and, provided that no possible source of pollution is shown, and the stream is vigorous, then there is no problem — you'll be enjoying 'mineral' water — free!

Organisation of the walks

There are 34 main walks in this book, spread across the entire Pyrenees (France, Spain and Andorra). Many are accessible by public transport, but for the more remote parts of the range the use of a car is essential. Ten walks are in the eastern Pyrenees and easily reached from the Costa Brava or Côte Vermeille; seven are in the western Pyrenees, for those based at resorts like Biarritz or San Sebastián; the remainder are spread among the high peaks between Andorra and the Pic d'Anie. Several walks cross the frontier, so have your passport with you (but there will only be an izard to look at it). For those with a little time, *all* the walks are accessible, since the chain is only 400km coast-to-coast, with an excellent motorway and railway system.

Begin by taking a look at the fold-out map and noting the walks that are nearest to you. Then turn to the route notes and the accompanying large-scale maps. Each walk is described in the direction we think the most attractive and that poses the least transport problems, but you may prefer the reverse direction. To help you get the 'feel' of the walk, there is at least one photo for each.

Every itinerary begins with planning information — distance, grade, how to get to and from the walk, etc. Pay particular attention if we refer to an ascent — 1000 metres is pretty tough going for the average walker. Times are given for reaching certain points in the walk, but bear in mind that everyone walks at a different speed ... and that personal speeds will vary according to the load carried, the weather, and the time of day. As a rule of thumb, reckon on 4km/h on a good track on the flat and add one hour for every 300m/1000ft of ascent. *No time is included for stops;* increase the times by *at least* one-third to allow for lunch stops, photography and nature-watching.

These symbols are used on the walking maps:

motorway	spring, waterfall, etc	specific building
main road	church.chapel	start/end.waypoint
secondary road	shrine or cross	ski lift
minor or untarred road	cemetery	quarry, mine.cave
track.path or trail	picnic place	stadium
main walk	best views	campsite
alternative	bus stop	map continuation
other walk	car parking	danger!
park boundary	railway station	prehistoric site
national boundary	ferry	power station
height in metres	castle, fort.watchtower	rock formation

Overnight accommodation

There are mountain *refuges* along some of our itineraries, offering refreshments, meals and very simple accommodation, usually in dormitories. None of the walks requires an overnight stop but, if you do stay overnight (for instance at the Refugio Góriz (Walk 26) or at Sarradets (Walk 22), then obviously you will have more time to enjoy the scenery and make side-trips. If you plan to spend a night at a refuge, it is preferable to take a sleeping bag, or at least a sleeping-bag liner — the blankets are a little unsavoury. *Always telephone ahead to make sure that the refuge is open, even in high summer.* And make sure that there are enough places — in high season the *refuges* can be a nightmare of recumbent bodies on floors and in corridors.

The French *gîte d'étape* is one grade above a refuge, but these are normally located in a hamlet or village on the valley floor, rather than on a mountaintop. *Gîtes* are good bases for those seeking budget accommodation and perhaps the *camaraderie* of fellow walkers and climbers.

Lightweight **camping** is generally possible in the high mountains, but note that some local authorities prohibit it. In the Spanish national parks (Aigües Tortes and Ordesa), bivouacs are only permitted at official sites; in the Parc National des Pyrénées (France), bivouacs must be at least 1km away from the roads.

Language hints

Throughout this book, names of places are given in the form in which they are most commonly seen locally and on walking maps (generally French names in France, Spanish names for most of the Spanish Pyrenees — but occasionally the Basque or Catalan form). Expect to see many variations — on maps, in guides, and on signposting! A short glossary of place name meanings is on page 44.

In case you become lost, you may have to ask the way. Here's one way to ask directions and understand the answers you get! First, memorise the few 'key' and 'secondary' questions shown overleaf. **Then, always follow up your key question with a second question demanding a yes or no answer.** Following are the two most likely situations in which you will have to practice your French or Spanish. The dots (...) show where you will fill in the name of your destination. We assume that you are familiar with the basics of French and Spanish pronunciation, but it's a good idea to ask a local person to help you with the pronunciation of place names.

Asking the way

The key questions

English	French	Spanish
Hallo.	Bonjour.	Buenos días.
I am lost.	Je me suis perdu.	Me he extraviado.
Please —	S'il vous plaît —	Por favor —
Where is	Où se trouve	Dónde está
the road to ... ?	la route de ... ?	la carretera a ... ?
the path to ... ?	le sentier de ... ?	la senda de ... ?
the bus stop?	l'arrêt d'autocar?	la parada?
the station?	la gare?	la estación?

Secondary questions leading to a yes/no answer

Is it here?	Est-ce (que c'est) ici?	Está aquí?
there?	là-bas?	allá?
straight ahead?	tout droit?	todo recto?
behind?	derrière?	detrás?
to the left?	à gauche?	a la izquierda?
to the right?	à droite?	a la derecha?
above?	en haut?	arriba?
below?	en bas?	abajo?
Thank you.	Merci.	Gracias.

Asking a taxi driver to take you somewhere and return for you, or asking a taxi driver to collect you somewhere:

English	French	Spanish
Please —	S'il vous plaît —	Por favor —
Take us to ...	Emmenez-nous à ...	Llévanos a ...
Come and pick us up at ... (place)	Venez nous chercher à ...	Venga buscarnos a ...
at ... (time) *	à ... *	a ... *

Instead of memorizing the hours of the day, simply point out on your watch the time you wish to be collected, or write it down.

Place name meanings (B: Basque; P: used throughout the Pyrenees)

ague, aigüe — water (P)
aran — valley (B)
arri — stone (B)
barranc, barranco — ravine (P)
bide — path (B)
borda — farmhouse (B)
borde — farm (P)
campana — rock 'needle' (P)
celhay — plateau (B)
chipi — small (B)
col, coll, collado — pass (P)
cortal — shepherd's hut (P)
coume — narrow valley (P)
cuby — bridge (B)
estany — pond, lake (P)
étang — pond (P)
erreka — stream (B)
etehola — hut (B)
farga — ancient forge (P)
font — spring (P)
gave — mountain torrent (P)
hourguette — steep pass (P)
iban — valley (B)
jasse — level pasture (P)
marcadau — market (P)
mendi — mountain (B)
orri, orrhy — stone hut (P)
pené — ridge (P)
prat — meadow (P)
río, riu — river (P)
val — valley (P)
zubi — bridge (B)

Walk 1: FROM VILAJUÏGA TO LLANÇÀ

Distance: 17.4km/10.8mi; 4h
Grade: ● moderate, with some 700m/2300ft of ascent; well signposted; PR- and GR-waymarked
Equipment: vegetation is prickly, so keep legs covered; strong footwear, water, picnic, swimming gear
Transport: 🚆 (RENFE 91 2 320 320; renfe.com) or 🚐 (Moventis SARFA 900 36 00 00; moventis.es) to Vilajuïga. Or 🚗: Car tour 1; park at Vilajuïga station (42° 19.495'N, 3° 5.186'E). Return by 🚆 from Llançà to Vilajuïga (RENFE)
Short walk: Park by the 'Cap de Creus' panel 0.8km beyond Vilajuïga (see below) and walk only as far as **Dolmen de la Carena**, returning by the same route (1h return).
Alternative walk: Holidaymakers staying in **Llançà** can follow the last GR 11 section of the walk backwards to **Sant Pere de Rodes** (❺), returning to Llançà by the same route (3h return).

This walk has everything — magnificent scenery, prehistoric remains, an important Romanesque monastery, a ruined castle, and a swim in the Mediterranean to cool off at the end of the hike.

From **Vilajuïga** STATION, **start out** (⭕) by walking under the bypass road and keeping straight on along the old main road, the Carretera de Roses. Then take the third left into the village. In the first square, PLAÇA MARGINEDA, there is an ancient synagogue (incorporated into Sant Feliu). Continue past the lovely white building on your right (AIGÜES MINERALS DE VILAJUÏGA, where, Mondays to Fridays, you can fill your water bottle at the spring).

Then turn right, following the road signposted 'ST PERE DE RODES'. Some 0.8km beyond the last house, where a large panel announces 'PARC NATURAL DE CAP DE CREUS' take the earthen track to the right, clearly signed 'MAS VENTÓS' (❶; **30min**).

Marked occasionally by YELLOW PR PAINT FLASHES, the track starts out with an olive grove to the left, then runs between a stream bed and another olive grove, after nine minutes (**39min**) becoming

St Pere de Rodes, and the ruined castle of Sant Salvador de Verdera above it. The first written reference to the beautiful monastery dates from the 9th century.

impassable to vehicles. Continue on a clearly-defined path for another eight minutes (**47min**) — to where another STREAM BED JOINS FROM THE LEFT. Cross the (normally dry) stream bed you have been following, to get onto an ascending path that keeps the new stream bed immediately to its left. After two minutes (**49min**) the path divides: go left and cross the new stream bed (there's a YELLOW PAINT FLASH to make it clear). In three minutes (**52min**) you will be at your first *dolmen*, the **Vinya del Rei** (**1** on the map), a stone burial chamber dating from approximately 5000 years ago. Having found your first *dolmen*, the next four are easy — roughly in line as you ascend the spine of the hill. In **56min**, come to **Dolmen del Garrollar** (to the right of the path; **2**), then **La Talaia** (**3**; **1h**), **Les Ruïnes** (**4**; **1h01min**) and **La Carena** (**5**; (**1h04min**). Continue climbing beyond La Carena and, in **1h09min**, just before you arrive on the tarmac road from Vilajuïga, you come to a sign, 'COVA DEL LLOP CAIGUTS I & II'. If you head right and take the path which plunges into the scrub, you can see these *dolmen* (**6** and **7**) and be back on the road again in 15 minutes (**1h25min**). Six minutes later (**1h31min**) another path to the right takes in **Vinyes Mortes I** (**8**) **and II** (**9**). Return to the road and continue for a further 10 minutes — to where a dirt track signposted 'MAS MARGALL' turns off to the left.

Follow the track to the ruined farm of **Mas Margall** (❷; **1h53min**), where you take the fork to the right, climbing above the *mas*. In another minute, where your track joins another, turn left. At the next divide, fork right and in 10 minutes cross the tarmac road and take the track almost directly opposite, signposted 'SANT ONOFRE'. In a hundred paces, your onward route, signposted 'SANTA HELENA, ST PERE DE RODES' is to the left; but first, if you like organised picnic spots, there are tables and benches under the pines at **Mas Ventós**, two minutes straight ahead (❸; **2h05min**).

Continuing, the well-trodden path climbs up to the **Serra de Santa Helena**, giving the opportunity to visit the ruined castle of **Sant Salvador de Verdera** (❹), the controversially restored monastery of **Sant Pere de Rodes** (❺), and the church of **Santa Helena** (❻) — they are best

Walk 1: From Vilajuïga to Llançà 47

approached in that order. From Santa Helena, follow the path northwards that descends to the road, continue northwards and, just after the junction signposted 'EL PORT DE LA SELVA', take the track signposted 'COLL PERER, LLANÇA' (**7**; **2h40min** (not including sightseeing!). This is also the **GR 11** and is marked with RED AND WHITE STRIPES. The track descends only slightly at first, northwards, but

Many farms are now in ruins.

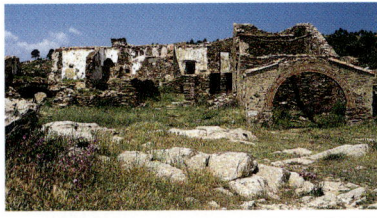

after eight minutes it begins to swing more to the right (northeast). After 15 minutes on this track, you pass a RUINED BARN about 200m/yds away to your right (**2h56min**) and continue up the hill towards a low RADIO MAST. The track curves to the left and then, quite unexpectedly, the red and white stripes direct you off the track, to the right (**3h**), along a much poorer path and over the SADDLE of the hill. From the saddle you descend eastwards. You drop down to a stone-built shepherd's '*orri*', almost concealed by vegetation, climb a little and then descend steeply into a low point, the signposted **Coll del Perer** (**8**; **3h10min**), a good area to spot red-legged partridges.

Ignore the path that climbs the hill straight ahead, as well as the one to the right that heads towards La Vall de Santa Creu, and instead turn left (north) along a gully for 'LLANÇA'. Some five minutes from the dip, come to a look-out point (**3h15min**) which makes a convenient place to take a break. Ahead of you are the church and white houses of Llançà, the higher Pyrenees (the Albères), and the coast stretching away to the border.

Continue on a clear path which descends to the little stream known as the **Rec d'en Prim** (dry in summer) and meander along until you reach the Les Esplanes area of **Llançà** at a large ROUNDABOUT (**3h45min**). From here take CARRER SANT PERE DE RODA, and make your way to the PLAÇA MAJOR (you'll see the church tower sticking up above the surrounding buildings). Here you can get a well-deserved drink and a taxi. To swim, walk down to the sea; for a train, leave the square in the direction of the main road and then cross the road to get to the STATION (**9**; **4h**).

Walk 2: FROM CADAQUES TO ROSES

Distance: 18.4km/11.4mi; 6h15min
Grade: ● quite easy; a fairly long walk, undulating between sea level and 300m/985ft); GR waymarking
Equipment: sturdy shoes, water, picnic, swimming gear
Transport: This walk begins with a 🚢 ferry ride from Roses, access by 🚌 (Moventis SARFA 900 36 00 00, moventis.es; SAGALES 902 13 00 14, sagales.com; or Alsa 902 42 22 42, alsa.es). Or 🚗: Car tour 1; park at the harbour at Roses (42° 15.068'N, 3° 10.909'E). Then 🚢 Don Pancho ferry (972 15 24 26, donpancho.org) from the harbour to Cadaqués. *Check the embarcation point in advance; it may be north of the harbour itself!*
Useful contacts: taxi: taxienroses. com or 670 38 85 12; Roses Tourist Office 972 25 73 31, visit roses.cat; Cadaques Tourist Office 972 25 83 15, visitcadaques.org
Short walk: Take the ferry from Roses as far as either **Cala Jóncols** or **Cala Montjoi** *(making clear that you wish to disembark there)* and walk back. The section from Cala Montjoi to the former *zona militar* is especially beautiful.
Alternative walk: Holidaymakers staying in Cadaqués may wish to do the walk in reverse, taking the ferry to Roses and walking back.

Cadaqués, made famous by the surrealist artist Salvador Dalí, who lived nearby, effortlessly combines bohemianism and sophistication. For this memorable day out, take the ferry to Cadaqués from the harbour at Roses and then walk back, pausing to swim along the way.

Begin the walk on the PASSEIG in **Cadaqués** (⊙), a cool, tree-lined square close to where the ferries dock. Follow the sea-front road southwards to the end of the village. Just beyond the Hotel Llane Petit the tarmac comes to an end. If you fancy a swim go left for the beach at Sa Conca, otherwise bear right on the signposted dirt track and almost immediately take the concrete path to the left. It's the first of several

Walk 3: From Cadaques to Roses

Top: landscape east of Roses in late spring; above: Dolmen de la Creu d'en Cobertella, easily reached from Roses

short-cuts (watch for yellow paint flashes), but essentially you will now be on dirt track almost all the way.

After about **25min** the track divides. Go right, climbing over a rock-slab surface and heading inland — the aim is to take a short cut across the peninsula, not to follow the coast. After another 25 minutes pass an isolated whitewashed house (MAS D'EN BALTRE) and, almost immediately, cross a STONE BRIDGE (**❶**; **50min**). At the narrow Y-fork beyond it, ignore the left-hand track. Go right instead, ascending (there may be an sign painted on a rock here advertising apartments at Cala Jóncols). As you climb, the Faro (lighthouse) de Cala Nans becomes briefly visible away to the left.

In **1h15min** ignore a track to the right (which goes towards Puig el Pení, with its unmistakable radar globes), and continue past a well-fenced house — to a HIGH POINT where the track divides (**1h40min**). Go right (the left fork is a private track to a house). As the views open out, you will see, far ahead, a track winding southwards; this is your onward route to Roses. Moments later, Cala Jóncols (possibly your first appointment with a swimming costume) appears far below. Keep straight ahead, ignoring two tracks to the right and descending to a junction with the TRACK FROM ROSES. Turn left and arrive at the beach and hotel at **Cala Jóncols** (**❷**; **3h**). It's hard to know what to do first, drink or swim.

When you are ready to continue the walk, climb the stone steps at the far end of the beach, and then turn left on a path which heads southeast. Five minutes from the beach (**3h05min**), bear right (ignoring the path to the left) towards the saddle and, and, once on the SADDLE, bear right again (ignoring another path to the left). The path now descends to a stream (dry in summer) and then climbs to the landward end of the **Cap de Norfeu**, where you regain the track (**❸**; **3h12min**). Ignore the track off left to the Torre de Norfeu (**❹**) — but you'll get some fine views there if you have the energy — and continue on down the track to swim at **Cala Montjoi** (**❺**; **4h15min**).

Now, from the far end of the beach, follow the footpath signed 'CAMÍ DE RONDA' (also the GR 92 footpath, occasionally marked by red and white stripes). This gorgeous section of footpath first runs below a museum dedicated to El Bulli (a Michlin restaurant once praised as the best in the world), then passes a tiny cove (**4h17min**), and **Cala Rostella** (**4h31min**) — to bring you into **Cala Murtra** (**❻**; **4h43min**), a naturist beach (do you dare?). Here be sure to cross the GULLY before looking for the path onwards, which climbs very steeply.

At **Punta Falconera** (**❼**; **5h**) you reach some ABANDONED BUNKERS in the old *zona militar*. The presence of the Spanish military here until the 1990s saved the point from development. Turn left on a track and almost immediately left again on a path that continues to follow the coast, eventually joining tarmac (**5h14min**).

You are now back in civilisation, but the coastal path will continue to delight. Soon you can descend steps from the road to Almadrava Beach (also known as **Canyelles Grosses**; **5h17min**), from where the path continues beside the sea to the fine sand beach of **Canyelles Petites** (**5h35min**) and then to the **Far de Roses** (**❽**; lighthouse; **5h57min**), from where you are obliged to follow the road back to the harbour at **Roses** (**❾**; **6h15min**).

Walk 3: FROM COLLIOURE TO BANYULS-SUR-MER

See also photo on page 13
Distance: 13km/8mi; 4h15min
Grade: ● easy underfoot — but involves 600m/1970ft of ascent; PR and GR/HRP waymarking
Equipment: sturdy shoes, picnic, water
Transport: 🚐 (lio-occitanie.fr, 08 06 80 03 50) or 🚆 (SNCF 36 35 within France or sncf-voyageurs.com) to Collioure; or 🚗: Car tour 1; park at Collioure, by the harbour (42° 31.339'N, 3° 5.078'E). Return by 🚐 or 🚆 from Banyuls-sur-Mer
Short walk: Follow the main walk to **Notre-Dame-de-Consolation** (❷) and return the same way (1h; ● easier ascent of 150m/490ft).

Here's a glorious high-level walk between two Côte Vermeille resorts with artistic claims to fame. Collioure was once the much-favoured summer haunt of the group of radical artists known as the Fauves ('wild beasts') because of their use of vivid and emotive colour and form. Among the more well-known members of the school were Matisse, Derain, Vlaminck and Rouault. Banyuls-sur-Mer was the birthplace and long-time home of world-famous sculptor Aristide Maillol.

Start out at **Collioure** by following the RUE DE LA REPUBLIQUE up from the harbour to the busy main road. Notice straight ahead, on the skyline, the Tour Madeloc, the highest point of the walk. Cross the main road by the ROUNDABOUT (⭕) and, almost directly opposite, take the RUE DU TEMPLE (signed to 'FORT ST-ELME'), passing under the RAILWAY LINE into the RUE DE LA GALÈRE and then the CHEMIN DE LA CONSOLATION.

At **14min**, at a narrow U-fork, take the road to the left signposted 'CONSOLATION'. This lane climbs gently through vineyards to the bypass flyover. Carry on under the FLYOVER, keeping left at a fork and keeping the stream to your left initially; then, after some 300 metres, cross the stream on a little BRIDGE (❶) to the opposite side. Just beyond the bridge take the left-hand fork and, a moment later, on the right, the distinctively cobbled

Approaching the Tour Madeloc through rock roses and gorse

old pilgrimage trail, marked 'ERMITAGE BAR/HOTEL'. The path, later concreted, climbs steeply to the SHRINE OF 'STE-ANNE' (**27min**), beyond which descend the tarmac road. Just before a sharp bend, take the stone steps on the left and, then, the little path that leads to the old hermitage of **Notre-Dame-de-Consolation** (**2**; **32min**), a favourite barbecue and boules spot. Telephone (01 43 80 46 93) if you would like to stay.

To continue, ignore the clear, wide path ahead; instead, ascend a few steps on the left and pass behind

52

a derelict building. After a steep, rocky climb, reach a RIDGE (**40min**) and ascend to the right (south). The path now runs amongst low scratchy bushes, climbing gently before zigzagging up to a wide tarmac road (D86; **3**; **1h05min**). Turn right, following YELLOW ARROWS for 450 metres, until you come to a long bend with low brick bollards; there take a track running obliquely back to the left, marked with the YELLOW PR SIGNPOSTS marking this walk. There is usually a metal barrier preventing vehicles using this track.

Climb to a saddle and ascend the steep ridge to the signposted **Batterie de Taillefer** (④; **1h45min**). Beyond this battery, the track merges in four minutes with another coming up from the left. After five metres, leave this vehicle track and take the well-maintained path to the right; it climbs gradually.

At **2h10min** an old watchtower comes into view and the path zigzags sharply up to it through some hairpin bends. The **Tour Madeloc** (⑤; **2h20min**) was built by James I of Mallorca at the end of the 13th century as part of a lookout/communication system. While the tower is closed to the public, the spectacular views remain — all along the Côte Vermeille and the Costa Brava, inland to the Col de Banyuls, and to another tower further west, the Tour de la Massane.

From the Tour Madeloc descend on a narrow tarmac road to another BATTERY (⑥; **2h40min**). Just beyond the main gates, take the narrow footpath indicated by a YELLOW SIGNPOST. The path itself may be marked with blue and white flashes. You drop down steeply

Maillol's La Pensée, *at his tomb near Banyuls (a short taxi journey from the front)*

towards Banyuls-sur-Mer, which you can see on the coast.

In five minutes you meet a path coming from the right. This is the famous **GR 10** (❼; **2h45min**), here combined with the more demanding Haute Route Pyrénées (**HRP**), the final leg of an adventure that for some will have begun over 400km away — at Hendaye on the Atlantic coast.

You will be following this path, marked clearly with RED AND WHITE FLASHES, down to the coast. At **2h50min** a vehicle track, also marked with red and white flashes, joins from the right, and you emerge on tarmac (again the D86, the 'CIRCUIT DE VIGNOBLE' — route of the vineyards).

Turn right along the road for 50 metres, then take a clear red-and-white-marked path on the left, short-cutting hairpin bends, to regain tarmac and reach a TABLE D'ORIENTATION (❽; **3h05min**). Beyond it, the road sweeps round to the right in a hairpin bend, but you continue straight ahead — on the right-hand, slightly higher of two earthen tracks. From here on the number of side-turnings is too great to show on the map or describe. Carefully follow the well-marked but convoluted GR on its descending course, at **3h40min** meeting a surfaced road. Turn left and, almost immediately, right. Very soon bear right on a signposted unmade vehicle track along a low ridge until, at **3h50min**, you reach a house with a 2m/6ft-high wire fence. Here you will see your path running between the vineyards.

Descend towards the RAILWAY LINE and pass through a TUNNEL underneath it (**4h**). Turn left for the RAILWAY STATION (ⓐ; signposted 'GARE'), otherwise continue straight ahead on the path along the gully which brings you out on AVENUE PUIG DEL MAS, one of the main streets in **Banyuls-sur-Mer**, at **4h05min**.

Turn left to the beach. Just before reaching the sea front, look out for a plaque on the building at the left (No 6) where the sculptor Maillol was born. The BUS STOP and taxis are on the seafront, to the right, in front of the Office de Tourisme (❾; **4h15min**). The RAILWAY STATION is close by and clearly signposted 'GARE'.

Walk 4: CIRCUIT IN THE GARROTXA, AND SANTA PAU

Distance: 17km/10.5mi; 3h45min
Grade: ● easy, except for the fairly steep climb of 200m/650ft to the rim of the Santa Margarida crater; natural park and GR waymarking
Equipment: sturdy shoes, water, picnic
Transport: 🚌 to Olot from Figueres (TEISA 972 26 01 96 or teisa-bus.com); then 🚕 taxi (682 63 94 35) to Can Serra, the parking area for the Fageda d'en Jordà; pre-arrange your return. Or 🚌 to Can Serra (42° 9.271'N, 2° 31.026'E): Car tour 2; about 3.5km southeast of Olot on the GI524, with a parking charge in summer).
Other useful numbers: Olot Tourist Office: 972 26 01 41, turismeolot.com; Park information: 972 26 60 12, en.turismegarrotxa.com; search for Fageda d'en Jorda; Casal de Volcans, 972 26 81 12
Short walk: Omit Santa Pau; continue directly to **Volcà de Santa Margarida** (❻) and **Volcà Croscat** (❼), saving 1h30min. (Be sure to visit Santa Pau by car afterwards.)

Behind the Costa Brava lies one of the most important volcanic regions in Europe, the Garrotxa. The earliest eruption was some 350,000 years ago, the most recent 11,500 years ago. Our walk takes you first through the Fageda d'en Jordà, a once-great beech wood, into this strange volcanic region which, with its curious light and lush vegetation, has long inspired artists such as Joaquim Vayreda, one of the founders of the Olot School.

Start out from the VISITORS' CENTRE at **Can Serra** (⊙). Take the underpass and follow a signposted path into the **Fageda d'en Jordà**. In summer you will be grateful for the shade of these marvellous trees. In **2min** reach another signpost. We are going to follow **PNZVG** (Parc Natural de la Zona Volcanica de la Garrotxa) **Circuit 1** as far as 'VOLCA STA MARGARIDA'.

Meander through the wood, following the signs, and in **16min** join a tarmac road. Turn right. In two minutes more (**18min**) pick up the red and white paint flashes of the **GR 2** and follow the road past the **Cooperativa La Fageda** (❶) to the beautiful old stone farmhouse shown left, **Prat de la Plaça** (❷; **28min**). Turn left on a track which runs along the side of the house, and 300m/yds further on, leave the track, taking a path to the right.

Left, top to bottom: the little church of Sant Miquel Sacot; Prat de la Plaça, an old stone farmhouse; the ermita *in the floor of the Volcà de Santa Margarida. Below: the beeches of the Fageda d'en Jordà. Bottom: in the Volcà Croscat (an easy detour on the return route)*

Walk 4: Circuit in the Garrotxa, and Santa Pau 57

Climb steadily over mud and steep rock, and finally through a gully between fields, to emerge on the brow of a hill overlooking the little church of **Sant Miquel Sacot** (❸; **40min**). Beyond it is the tree-clad cone of Santa Margarida.

Descend to the CHURCH on tarmac, and from there follow the sign *'VOLCA STA MARGARIDA'*. Your track (initially surfaced) passes to the right of the church. Almost immediately, descend a rough, steep path to the right — a short-cut only marked with a waymarking post when last seen. At the bottom of the hill you emerge on signposted track again (**45min**); turn right to a junction, where you turn right again and pass a SHRINE on the left. After a further couple of minutes come to a major junction. Ignore tracks to left and right: choose the lesser (narrower) track ahead.

At the top of this ascent (**50min**) cross a good track and keep ahead on a lesser one, to continue in the same direction. You pass a 3m/10ft-high 'cliff' of eroded ash, an indication that you are now ascending the cone of Margarida. By **57min** follow signs for *'SANTA MARGARIDA, SANTA PAU'*. After another minute, a sign directs you left to the cone of Margarida.

A minute or so later the TRACK DIVIDES (❹; **1h**). For now ignore the crater (up to the left) and continue ahead for Santa Pau, skirting a FARM (**1h05min**), and joining a track where a sign soon directs you to the left for SANTA PAU. In 40 minutes you can be enjoying the medieval centre of **Santa Pau** (❺; **1h45min**) and a drink in one of the cafés.

Refreshed, retrace your steps back to the JUNCTION you reached 1h into the walk (❹) and climb the zigzag path through dense forest to the RIM of the **Volcà de Santa Margarida**. Then descend to the ERMITA shown opposite (❻; **2h45min**). Relax, the last eruption in the area was 11,500 years ago (...on the other hand, experts have deduced that the cycle of activity is 10,000 years!).

Climb back to the rim of the crater and take the clearly signposted track for *'VOLCA DEL CROSCAT'*. This descends the north side of the cone, crosses the road to the RESTAURANT SANTA MARGARIDA, and passes around the north side of **Volcà Croscat** (❼). You are now back on **PNZVG Circuit 1**: follow signs to *'FAGEDA D'EN JORDA'*, to regain the large **Can Serra** CAR PARK in one hour (**3h45min**).

If you have the time, once back in Olot, visit the Casal dels Volcans, which explains the geology of the region, and the Museu Comarcal, which features the work of many of the artists it has inspired.

Walk 5: SANT ANIOL D'AGUJA

See also the lower photo on page 62
Distance: 16km/10mi; 4h21min
Grade: ●❗ moderate, with an ascent of about 500m/1650ft; some slippery sections and river crossings; PR/GR waymarking
Note and **warning**: *On rare occasions (after prolonged heavy rain) the Sant Aniol river bed may be* **impassable**.
Equipment: no special equipment, but be prepared for wet feet. See notes on 'Walking', page 38.
Transport: 🚗 (Car tour 2). Just east of Castellfollit de la Roca take the road GIP5233 for Montagut and then Sadernes. The tarmac turns to dirt track in the hamlet of Sadernes. The track beyond Sadernes is closed to vehicles from March 15th to September 30th. If you come in summer you are thus obliged to use the car park just past the church (42° 16.161'N, 2° 35.610'E). In winter you have the option of driving along the track a little beyond the Pont d'en Valenti, which will save a total of 6km/3.8mi; 1h30min (see map).
Shorter walk: to Sant Aniol (**⑤**), then retrace steps (12.5km/7.8mi; 3h 40min; ● moderate; ascent 150m/490ft)

An astonishing lesson in social history. As you enjoy your holiday trek, not hard but invigorating, you are following the traditional everyday routes of country folk, past a chapel and through villages now long deserted.

We start our timings from the CAR PARK (**◯**) just past the CHURCH in **Sadernes**. Drop down to the track and follow the signs for 'SANT ANIOL' (upstream). When you reach the **Pont d'en Valenti** (**❶**; **40min**), do not cross it. Continue instead to a place where you can traverse the bed of the **Riera** (river) **de Sant Aniol** (**❷**; **56min**).

It may be dry at this point, or you may have to use stepping stones — or even take off your boots and paddle (depending on the season). Almost immediately afterwards, there *may* be a sign pointing to 'TALAIXA', up a track to the left. But you continue *straight ahead*, until you are surrounded by the open fields of the farm of **La Muntada** (**1h10min**). Leave the track (which crosses the river) and continue straight ahead on a narrow path which in two minutes brings you to a little WEIR (**❸**; **1h12min**). Pick your way across the top of the wall. You are now entering the dramatic canyon section of the walk. The path hugs the left bank of the stream (ie, the stream is on your left), and you pass deep clear pools offering many summer bathing possibilities.

After **1h29min** the path divides. Either veer left to the river and cross on stepping stones or veer right and two minutes later (**1h31min**) scramble down water-smoothed rocks and cross by an 'Indiana Jones' narrow plank and log bridge. This is an excellent bathing spot. You are now on the river's right bank, but just a moment later (**1h33min**) cross over to the left bank once again by barely adequate stepping stones. You'll see an OPEN AREA WITH A RUIN AHEAD of you. Turn left and continue along the river.

Eventually you reach a junction with the **GR 11** (**❹**; **1h36min**), with red and white paint flashes. Follow the GR to the left, along the same river as before. At **1h41min** there is another divide, but you continue to climb through box woods and past flat fields on the GR.

By **1h44min** you are down by

Talaixà: take the time for the five minute walk up to the church.

the river again which you cross by stepping stones; very soon the hermitage and chapel of **Sant Aniol** (**❺**; **1h50min**) appear just above you, built in the 11th century in the Romanesque style on a 9th-century site. The old refuge behind, once derelict, is being restored as a walkers' hostel — as money permits. Climb up and perhaps picnic here.

Go to the **Font** (spring) **de Sant Aniol** (straight ahead of you when you stand with your back to the entrance to the refuge).* Take the path to the right of the *font* but, behind the *font,* turn left and follow the footpath across a usually dried-up river bed and through woods of giant sweet chestnut trees. There are plenty of side paths here, so keep checking for the red and white stripes of the GR 11. You climb continuously and after 15 minutes pass through a swing-close GATE WITH GR MARKINGS (**2h05min**). At **2h10min** a vertiginous drop to your left gives spectacular VIEWS of the river below and across heavily-wooded mountain wilderness to the summit of Bassegoda in the northeast (1373m/4505ft). The path swings westwards and passes a large BOULDER (**2h23min**) on which a painted sign indicates that Talaixà is straight ahead. At **2h28min** pass through another self-closing gate.

When you reach the ruined hamlet of **La Quera** (**❻**; **2h37min**) you may well wonder — just how did they get anything to this spot? Look around for your onward marking: you'll see it at the back of the hamlet, leading on up the valley, between the wall of a house and a hedge.

After another 13 minutes of steady climbing and faithfully following GR waymarks, you arrive at **Talaixà** (**❼**; **2h50min**), a ruined hilltop hamlet with a 17th-century church and views east and west over paradise.

You *leave* the GR here to descend sharply left from the path you arrived on, going back down the same valley — but on the opposite side. There may be limited YELLOW WAYMARKS here — *no* red and white GR marks. Watch out for loose stones on this twisty and gravelly

---

*Before continuing to Talaixà, you could take a 30min (return) detour from the *font* to the signposted 'Salt del Brull' waterfall (**ⓐ**).

60 Landscapes of the Pyrenees

descent. At **3h35min** you reach the river again. Don't cross it; instead, follow a footpath running along the right-hand side of the river.

Then you come to **Easy Day**, a New Age retreat and education centre with a café, and the lovely **Pont d'en Valenti** FOOTBRIDGE (**❶**; **3h39min**). Cross and ascend to your outgoing track (**3h41min**). Turn right and return to the CAR PARK (**4h21min**).

Walk 6: THE ALTA GARROTXA AND SANTA BÀRBARA DE PRUNERES

See map opposite
Distance: 14km/8.7mi; 4h
Grade: ● moderate, with an ascent of about 350m/1150ft; some descending sections are littered with loose stones. PR and GR waymarking
*Note and **warning**: On rare occasions (after prolonged heavy rain) the Sant Aniol river bed may be **impassable**.*
Equipment: walking boots (see notes on 'Walking', page 38.

Transport: 🚗 (Car tour 2). Just east of Castellfollit de la Roca, take the road GIP5233 for Montagut and continue to the hamlet of Sadernes, where there is a car park just past the church (42° 16.161'N, 2° 35.610'E).

Short walk: Walk only as far as **Coll de Jou** (❶) for the spectacular views and return the same way (4km/2.5mi; 1h40min; ● lesser ascent/descent of 200m/650ft

The word '*garrotxa*' indicates a rugged landscape, where walking is difficult. Surprisingly, Bassegoda, the highest point of this spectacular region of Alta Garrotxa, is only 1373m/4505ft, but the narrow, steep-sided valleys are tremendously deep. This itinerary provides uplifting views all over this tortured region, including Puig de Bassegoda, and makes a tranquil alternative to the popular Sant Aniol walk (Walk 5).

Start the walk at the CAR PARK just past the church at **Sadernes** (⊙): a short way along the track take the downward path signposted 'OIX' and 'COLL DE PALOMERES'. After **12min** the path crosses the bed of the **Sant Aniol River** (normally dry, but you may have to rock-hop or paddle). Look out for a large rock on the far bank with the word 'OIX' painted on it. The path you want is *on top* of the rock and climbs steeply through evergreen oak woods.

The path reaches the **Coll de Jou** (❶; **50min**) where there is a little stone-built house. Skirt the house, cross the pasture, and turn right (westwards) to pass through the col. From here there are imposing views ahead of the cliffs along the Beget Valley in the northwest, as well as of Santa Bàrbara de Pruneres, nestling close to the summit ridge of the **Serra de Santa Bàrbara**.

At **1h** turn right on a track and follow it for just two minutes (**1h02min**) before turning right once more on a NARROW PATH (❷) MARKED BY CAIRNS. Soon you will have a clear view of the strangely-shaped Bassegoda in the northeast — looking like a bun on which someone has carelessly added an extra blob of dough.

At **1h18min**, just before a ruined house, swing leftwards and make your way up the grassy terraces to the 10th-century **Santa Bàrbara de Pruneres** (❸; **1h27min**). From the church follow the track which begins by heading northwards. Once clear of the woods there are splendid views westwards over the little village of Oix. Soon after the track passes a large FARMHOUSE, at a junction, turn left (**1h35min**), curling back southwards. At **1h47min**, at another junction, carry straight on towards a RED-TILED FARMHOUSE. At **1h50min** pass the house (**Palomeres**) and at **1h53min** reach yet another junction on the **Coll de Palomeres**, with a choice of two parallel tracks to the left. You want the first (*lower*) of these tracks, which is the **GR 1** (❹) footpath and occasionally marked by red and white stripes.

61

Above: in summer the Riera de Sant Aniol at Sadernes is dried up. If you reach this point in the river bed, you have gone too far north. Retrace your steps, looking for the rock with the word 'Oix' painted on it. At other times of the year the river flows nicely, as here (left) at the Pont d'en Valenti (Walk 5).

At **2h**, just beyond an opening in the forest, the way becomes a narrow path once more. Pass a RUIN at **2h13min** and a minute later turn right (eastwards) on a track. At **2h26min**, just after a chain, come to a junction and continue straight ahead. At **2h37min** leave the track, on a path bearing off to the right, and clearly marked with red and white stripes.

The path skirts the little shrine known as the **Oratori de Plansalloses** (❺; **2h40min**). In **2h55min** the path widens to a track and descends to the tarmac road at

the 12th-century stone footbridge, the **Pont de Llierca** (❻; **3h**) — a miracle of medieval engineering. Water to drink is available from the *font* across the road from the car park; water to swim in is reached by steps — *but not if the current is strong.*

Cross the bridge and turn left on a good track, soon reaching the prehistoric site of **La Bauma del Serrat del Pont** (❼). Continue on to a gate (**3h20min**), walk through a field past ruins, and descend to a FORD (usually dry; ❽; **3h35min**). Cross, ascend to the road and turn right to return to your car in **Sadernes** (**4h**).

Walk 7: A CANIGOU CANTER

Distance: 14km/9mi
Grade: 🔴 moderate, with some scrambling and an ascent of 1,200m/4,000 ft
Equipment: mountain walking equipment appropriate to the season and the altitude. See notes on 'walking', page 38.
Transport: This is a hike for which a car is essential, either your own, or a rental. Take the D618 north from Amélie-les-Bains for 22km and, at the Col Xatard turn left on the D13 to 'Valmanya' (another 17km). At Valmanya, go straight ahead to 'Els Masos de Valmanya' where the D13 goes left. There is a dedicated car park for walkers to Canigou (42° 31.863'N, 2° 31.147'E).
Shorter/Alternative walk: Turn around at the refuge known as the **Chalet des Cortalets** (③; 04 68 96 36 19, refugedescortalets.ffcam.fr), with its hostel-type accommodation, refreshments and meals (open summer only) for a total time of around 6 hours. In summer you may choose to enjoy a meal before descending or even to spend the night — to relax before the assault on the summit (and that is the way we have done our timings).

Canigou is the sacred mountain of the Catalans, the highest in the area at 2784m (9130 feet) with fabulous views over the mountains and the coast. Until recently it was possible to drive much of the way on a dirt track but for environmental reasons that is no longer allowed.

Our adventure begins at the PARKING AREA at the hamlet of **Els Masos** just beyond the village of Valmanya. In the northerly corner of the car park, a GR36 signpost for 'PRAT CABRERA (PAR PATRIQUES)' sets you on your way (it is also signed to the 'Refuge des Cortalets' and 'Pic du Canigou'. Follow the red and white flashes, and soon you are climbing through the impressive beech forest known as the **Bosc de Patriques** to emerge on a ridge and meet the **Route Forestière du Llech**, a motorable track. Admire the view from the lookout, then pass through a gate to skirt a flat area with a little hut known as the **Cabane de Prat Cabrera** (**1h45min**).

From here you will be on the merged GR10/GR36 footpaths, still

St-Martin-du-Canigou, near Walk 7 and Car tour 2

with the same waymarking. Leave the track and continue ahead. You will pass through a riot of rhododendrons, areas of scree and the wreck of a plane out of Gatwick that crashed in 1961, to reach the **Chalet des Cortalets** (❸; **3h15min**) a substantial refuge at 2150m/7053ft that was a Second World War hideout for the Maquis. In summer (end May to mid-October) you might like to reward yourselves for all that effort with a nice meal or even stay the night. Note that a reservation is essential (see details under 'Shorter/Alternative walk' on page 63. In winter you can still use the Cortalets for shelter but there will be no staff and no facilities at all, not even water.

Some 15 minutes beyond the Cortalets your footpath skirts a LAKE, leaving it to the left, and ascends westwards to the long ridge that leads to the summit. After 25 minutes you reach the **Fontaine de la Perdrix** (❹), a useful picnic spot and water source. You are no longer on the GR10 here.

In 55min you come to the bottom of the final ridge. A clear path leads past large rock formations with views towards the rubble-strewn east face.

Reach the BASE OF THE SUMMIT CONE (❺) in **1h10min**. From here a rocky path zigzags up to the top. Take care as it is steep and can be slippery. A final effort and you are on the SUMMIT of the sacred mountain, the **Pic du Canigou** (❻; **1h45min — 5h** from Els Masos), with wonderful views in every direction. The *table d'orientation* identifies the main summits.

Make your way back to the car park by the route you came up (**9h**).

Descending from the summit in springtime can be exhilarating — or very dangerous, if you haven't the right equipment. Be sure to read the notes on high-level walking before you tackle any of the peaks.

Walk 8: CARANÇA CLIFFHANGER

Distance: 20.7km/12.8mi; 7h40min
Grade: ●! moderate, but the climb of 1000m/3280ft demands considerable stamina
Equipment: good footwear is essential and a compass/gps might prove useful on the return leg in poor visibility — see introductory notes on 'Walking', page 38.
Transport: 🚂 (Petit Train Jaune) to Thuès-entre-Valls (the line runs from Villefranche-de-Conflent to Latour-de-Carol): for information telephone 00 68 05 41 02, letrainjaune.f; or 🚗 (Car tour 3). From Puigcerda take the D66 towards Perpignan and park in the car park below the railway station (42° 31.389'N, 2° 13.277'E).
Useful information: Prades Tourist Office 04 68 05 41 02; tourisme-canigou.com/organisez/voir-faire/randonnees/les-gorges-de-la-caranca
Short walks: Follow the main walk as far as the BALCONY (**2**; 27min), but instead of then turning left, turn right to return to the car park in a

total of 1h; or, for a slightly longer version, continue on the main itinerary until the FIRST OF THE LADDERS (**3**; 53min), from where you can return to the car park along the river's right bank in a total of 1h40min.
Alternative walks: ●! Once at the Refuge de la Carança you could simply return along your outward route, saving half an hour. But if you are super-fit, you could continue up to the **Etang de la Carança** (**a**); add 9.7km/6mi; 3h return, with an additional ascent/descent of 420m/1380ft.

Few walks offer such dramas within so short a distance of the car park — a narrow gorge, spectacular rock formations and gravity-defying walkways. And that's just the start!

Begin the walk at **Thuès** by passing under the RAILWAY BRIDGE at the end of the CAR PARK (**O**), just downhill from the station. Immediately you are in the bottom of a narrow gorge, whose sheer, high walls are a promise of vertiginous thrills to come.

In **10min** you have a choice: you can turn right and cross the BRIDGE (**1**) to follow our itinerary, but if you really have no head for heights, you can continue straight ahead to rejoin the main walk at the FIRST LADDER (**3**; the 53min-point). Beyond the bridge the path climbs to a BALCONY (**2**; **27min**). Turn left

(south) to continue the walk (but by turning right you can make a circuit back to the car park, with a total time of just under one hour). After thirty paces ignore the path that climbs up to the right (your return route).

Your onward path has been cut into the rock face with the raging waters of the **Carança Gorge** now dizzyingly far below — take a good grip on the hand rail! The balcony runs more or less horizontally until, after 26 minutes, you begin to negotiate a dazzling series of LADDERS AND BRIDGES (**3**; **53min**). This continues for just over an hour,

You'll need a good head for heights to follow this route through the Carança Gorge

after which you emerge from the gorge (**1h55min**).

A clear path now remains close to the river, climbing easily as the valley gradually opens out. At **3h** take careful note of a THREE-WAY SIGNPOST (❹) and a path that climbs back to your right (north); this is the return route. But for now carry on the extra 30 minutes to the **Refuge de la Carança** (❺; **3h30min**), where in summer refreshments await you.

The refuge is a walkers' crossroads. The GR 10 long distance footpath passes by, coming from the distinctive U-shaped col to the northwest (Coll Mitja) and crossing over the river in the direction of Mantet to the east. The celebrated Etang (Lake) de la Carança lies an hour and a half further south along the Carança River (Alternative walk — if you have the energy).

To return, retrace your steps to the CAIRN (❹; **4h**) and take the path to the left. It climbs in hairpins away from the river and then traverses the slope to the **Las Tours** stream (❻; **4h33min**). Cross the stream and continue past an *orri*. Some 15 minutes after the stream, leave a startling ROCK NEEDLE to your right

(**4h48min**). After another 17 minutes the path swings west to cross the **Roig** stream (❼; **5h05min**), then climbs in hairpins amongst hazel and mountain pine before redescending to another stream. Once across, leave another *orri* to your right.

At **5h55min**, where the path abruptly cuts back towards the southwest, the little **Dona Pa** REFUGE (❽; unstaffed) is just off to the right. After 10 minutes (**6h05min**) the path swings round to the north once more — ignore the path to the left. Your path now zigzags down through oak woods (used in the construction of the 'little yellow railway') to rejoin your outward route (**7h20min**). Turn left.

After 30 paces, at ❷, you will see the path you ascended from the first bridge seven hours earlier dropping down to your right. But we are not yet finished with the spectacle. Continue ahead along a path with terrifying drops to the right (you're used to them by now) and beautiful views out to the Têt Valley. Once clear of the gorge, the path winds down to the car park in **Thuès** (**7h40min**).

Walk 9: FROM NURIA TO QUERALBS

Distance: 16km/10mi; 6h20min
Grade: 🔴❗ moderate. In the main, the walk is a descent of some 750m/2460ft from Núria. Some GR waymarking in the first half of the walk, but mostly cairned
Note: This is a region savaged by winter weather, and although the local authorities attempt to maintain safe river crossings, they do not always succeed. Bridges swept away by avalanches may be replaced by makeshift log crossings or by nothing. You must take special care here and bear in mind that finding suitable crossings may add substantially to walk times.
Equipment: see introductory notes on 'walking', page 38.

How to get there: 🚆 to Ribes de Freser and then onwards by 🚋 *cremallera* — rack railway — to Núria. Or 🚗 (Car tour 2). From Ripoll head north to Ribes de Freser and then on up to Queralbs to catch the 🚋 *cremallera* there, rather than Ribes, because this is where the walk ends. Departures are at roughly hourly intervals in the high season but every two hours in the low season. The ascent takes 40 minutes. For all information on trains to Ribes, telephone RENFE 91 2 320 320 or see timetables online at renfe.com. For all information on the *cremallera*, telephone 972 73 20 20; valdenuria.cat.

Walk 9: From Nuria to Queralbs 69

Alternative walk: Follow the walk in the opposite direction: head downhill from **Queralbs** STATION (**8**) and turn left over a BRIDGE in five minutes. Immediately beyond this bridge fork left up a concrete track which leads to HYDROELECTRIC BUILDINGS (**7**). Cross a second bridge to reach these buildings and then turn right to enter the **Gorges del Freser**. Penetrate as far as you wish. ● Easy to moderate, depending on how far you climb.

The adventure begins with a ride on the *cremallera* (rack railway; the last to function commercially in Catalonia) from either Ribes or the little stone-built mountain village of Queralbs. The steep track passes high cliffs, runs along the edge of deep chasms and penetrates rock-hewn tunnels, before depositing its load of passengers and goods at the terminus. This is Núria (1967m/6450ft), Catalonia's first international ski station and site of the Santuari de Núria, where some of the traditionally ecclesiastical buildings have now been converted into a three-star hotel.

To start the walk at **Núria**, cross the RAILWAY LINE (**O**) and take the red/white waymarked **GR 11.7** (CAMI DELS ENGINYERS), keeping the top lift station above you to the left and

the cliff drop to the railway to your right. You ascend past some unusual religious sculptures, after **10min** swinging left. In **20min** you'll see on your left a large concrete altar with a GIANT CROSS (**1**) suspended above it. Stand on the track with your back to this and descend straight across pastureland (southeast, in the direction of the long part of the cross) — to a small footpath.

Follow this narrow earthen path over a shoulder and into a new vista — first bearing away towards the left to cross a stream and then southwards, cutting across the hillside towards a ridge. You reach a CAIRN ON THE RIDGE (**2**; **1h**); here the path turns sharp left, continuing more or less on the same contour, gradually joining a path rising from a shepherd's ruined hut *(orri;* **a***).* Watch for the occasional bemused izard (Pyrenean chamois), curious at the sight of walkers slithering downhill. The path leads away from the Gorges de Núria and into the awesome **Gorges del Freser**.

You cross the **Torrent de Coma de Gispet** (**4**; **1h25min**), then the path cuts a clear line across steep slopes, rising and falling, its surface alternating from loose stone to firmer rock. CAIRNS mark the way where necessary. For those with a hankering to yodel, this is a good spot, as the echoing calls of the chocards (choughs) demonstrate.

At **2h20min**, after a succession

Fire salamander

Núria

of often vertiginous views, you encounter the STEEPEST DESCENT of the walk. Follow the path close to the cliff. There is a CABLE HANDRAIL to assist you on the more vertiginous stretches. At **2h35min** mount the last in a series of small rises and climb through a gap between rock 'teeth', the **Cingles de la Balma**, to arrive at a wide grassy COL giving views on a new landscape.

The path turns sharp left and climbs to a ridge, which you reach at about **2h50min**. The path is now clear and well-marked with cairns. At **3h** you mount a small rise to see the modern and comfortable **Refugi Coma de Vaca** (**5**; 1995m/6544ft) where, a few minutes later, you can be enjoying a cool drink and, if you wish, a meal (34 872 98 70 98).

From the area of the refuge, paths go off in all directions, but their exact positions can change from year to year due to snow damage. You now want to *leave* the GR 11.7 and take the path through the bottom of the **Gorges del Freser** to Queralbs; this descends from the refuge to the **Riu Freser** and crosses by a small BRIDGE (at time of writing). A MARSHY SIDE-STREAM, crossed twice, poses the next obstacle, crossed where the ground is firm enough to pass.

Descend westwards on a clear path with fabulous views of the sheer rock faces you negotiated all the way from the ruined *orri*. You reach the VALLEY FLOOR in **4h35min**. Cross the **Riu Freser** again via a BRIDGE (**6**; Pont de les Marrades) or STEPPING STONES.

The walk now continues by following the clear path along the bottom of the valley, descending and crossing numerous streams. If it is evening, watch out for the nocturnal black and yellow fire salamanders, newt-like creatures so slow-moving that they run the risk of being trampled underfoot.

When you reach a HYDRO-ELECTRIC COMPLEX (**7**; **6h**), turn left over a bridge in front of it, to walk the short section of concrete track to the tarmac Queralbs/Ribes road (**6h10min**). Turn right for the short climb to **Queralbs** STATION (**8**; **6h20min**).

Walk 10: PEDRAFORCA

See also photos on pages 8-9, 17
Distance: 9km/5.6mi; 4h
Grade: ●! difficult; a strenuous ascent/descent (sometimes over scree) of 1072m/3516ft over a distance of just 4.5km/2.8mi. PR waymarking to the *Enforcadura*
Equipment: mountain walking equipment: you will ascend to 2498m/8193ft — see 'Walking' on page 38. Plenty of water — *there is no water on the mountain;* hiking poles; gloves for the scree descent
Transport: 🚗 to Gósol: Car tour 3; park in the square in the centre (42° 14.231'N, 1° 39.611'E), with a bar/restaurant. 🚌 A limited bus service between Gosol and Berga is run by bus company Alsa, 910 207 007, alsa.es.
Useful contacts: Oficina del Parc Natural del Cadí-Moixeró 938 244 151 or parcsnaturals.gencat.cat/en/xarxa-de-parks/cadi/index.html; Gósol *ajuntament* (town hall) 973 37 00 55, gosol.ddl.net

Short walk: Pla de la Serra (4.6km/2.9mi; 1h25min); ● quite easy ascent/descent of 450m/1475ft if taken slowly; follow the main walk to the **Pla de la Serra** (❷) and retrace steps.

Alternative walk: El Collell (8.8km/5.5mi; 3h45min); ● easy ascent/descent of about 450m/1475ft. Follow the **GR 107** (CAMÍ DELS BONS HOMES) to the picnic spot at **Coll de Font Terrers** (ⓐ; **45min;** also accessible by car — see Car tour 3) and from there via the **Font de la Roca** (ⓑ) to **El Collell** (ⓒ; **2h;** 1845m/6052ft), for its glorious views, returning the same way. PR and GR waymarking throughout. Join the footpath by taking CARRER PICASSO from the square (Plaça Major), and then CARRER DE LA CERDANYA.

Pedraforca (the name means forked rock) is one of the most famous mountains in Catalonia. Inside the beautiful Cadí-Moixeró Natural Park, the bizarre double summits, separated by a so-called *enforcadura* (fork) of scree, are a landmark challenging you to reach the summit. And, improbable as it may seem from the valley floor, you can! There are three main approaches. We are going to take you up the one that poses the least difficulty, which starts from Gósol. Do not let anybody convince you otherwise.

Set off from the fountain SQUARE (○) at the centre of **Gósol** (where a plaque on a house commemorates a stay by Picasso). Amble along the CARRETERA GUARDIO in the direction of Saldes, with the restaurant Cal Paraire to our left. Beyond the church, you will see the unmistakable Pedraforca off to your left and, in the foreground, TWO HOUSES a little separated from the village (shown in the photograph below). Just before the roundabout, take the road on the left and head towards those houses. The route is well marked by yellow and white flashes, all the way to the *Enforcadura* — if you go very far without seeing these footpath signs, you have lost your way.

At **5min** turn right, pass the houses and climb a gentle farm track. When the track runs out, swing to the right to cross the (normally dry) stony bed of the **Rubinat** stream (❶; **21min**). Now a path climbs steeply eastwards through the delightful pine woods on the flanks of the **Serra de la Tossa**, to emerge at the **Pla de la Serra** (❷; **55min**), a lovely clearing, with beautiful views from here over Gósol to the Serra del Cadí. *(The Short walk turns back here.)*

Continue straight across the clearing, back into the woods, and along the spine. The going gets even tougher when the path emerges from the wood on scree — the infamous **Tartera de Gósol** (❸; **1h05min**). If you have hiking poles, deploy them now. This loose stone is how it's going to be all the way to the *Enforcadura*. But there is a clear path and, surprisingly, the going gets a little easier towards the top, where tufts of grass glue the scree down and provide footholds. Keep your spirits up — you're quite likely to see izards (Pyrenean chamois).

At **2h** you reach the TOP OF THE **Enforcadura** (❹). The main summit (Pollego Superior) is to your left (north), and if you've made it this far, you can certainly make it

Walk 10: Pedraforca 73

all the way. From here on there are *no markings* at all, but you will see a faint path climbing up into the rocks where the boots of thousands of hikers have polished footholds and left clear traces. What looks from the valley like smooth rock is, in fact, a jumble of boulders which you can scramble up to reach the SUMMIT, **Pollego Superior** (❺; **2h25min**).

Congratulations! You are standing at 2498m/8193ft and, with sheer drops all around, it feels like it!

On no account think of making a circuit by descending to the Collada de Verdet — it is an exposed and highly dangerous descent.

When you have finished taking in the awesome views, go back down to the *Enforcadura* (❹;

the scree, but console yourself with the thought that the Tartera de Saldes, the opposite side of the *Enforcadura*, is even worse. Initially seek out the grassy tufts, and lower down use the deeper scree to the side of the path. Turning your feet sideways across the path also helps. Inevitably you will slip down a few times and will use your gloves.

At **3h15min** the scree is behind you, and 15 minutes later you can be relaxing back at the **Pla de la Serra** (❷; **3h30min**) before your return to **Gósol** (**4h**).

Left and above left: Pedraforca from Gósol and the start of the walk (the itinerary passes close to the two houses in the photograph on the left). The 'collar' of scree, the Enforcadura, *is clearly visible below the peaks. Top right: cathedral at La Seu d'Urgell, a good base for exploring the Cadí*

Walk 11: ENGOLASTERS AND THE MADRIU VALLEY

See also photo on page 1
Distance: 18km/11.2mi; 5h30min
Grade: 🔴 moderate, involving only 550m/1800ft of ascent; GR waymarking
Equipment: You'll be reaching over 2000m/6560ft; clothing must be appropriate to the conditions — see notes on 'Walking', page 38.
Transport: 🚌 to Les Escaldes (Cooperativa interurbana Andorrana 376 806 555), then 🚕 taxi (376 863 000, or turisandorra.com/taxi-en-andorra) to the lovely Romanesque church of Sant-Miquel d'Engolasters. Continue *past* the church towards the Estany (lake) d'Engolasters, and park at the final hairpin bend just before the lake (by a sign on the right, 'Circuit de les Fonts'). Pre-arrange a taxi for your return. Or 🚗: follow the notes for taxis to park at the hairpin bend (42° 31.059'N, 1° 34.256'E).
General information: Tourist Office of Escaldes-Engordany 376 890 881, visitandorra.com/en

Stroll: 🔵 Allow 1h30min for this easy 'figure-of-eight'. From the parking area continue uphill to the HOTEL-RESTAURANT and from there descend to the **Estany d'Engolasters**. Take the path below the dam and circle the lake, passing a couple of other bar/restaurants on the north side. Opposite the dam wall go left up the footpath with wooden railings, then return to the parking area. Now follow the main walk, taking time to climb up to the MIRADOR (with a plaque naming all the peaks around Andorra la Vella). Continue as far as the **Font dels Corralets**, then turn back. After three minutes turn sharp left down a path signposted 'CIRC. ESPORTIU'. This lovely grassy path rejoins the main track just short of the first *font*. Retrace your steps to the parking.

Short walk: 🔵 Follow the main walk to **Fontverd** (7) or just past **La Farga** (8) and return the same

Walk 11: Engolasters and the Madriu Valley 75

way (2h30min-4h, depending on where you turn round).
Alternative walk: ● From the **Refugi del Riu dels Orris** (**9**), continue on the **GR 7** to the **Refugi de l'Illa** (**a**; 2485m/ 8150ft) and the nearby lake, **Estany de l'Illa** (**b**; 2510m/8233ft). Worth the extra effort, but allow an extra 1h30min up, and at least 3h to get back to your car/taxi (7h30min in total).

Many of the larger Andorran valleys have been ruined by roads, building and ski development. This is one that, for now, remains beautifully unspoiled — a complete contrast to the hubbub of urban Andorra.

Start out from the 'CIRCUIT DE LES FONTS' SIGNPOST (○) near the **Estany d'Engolasters** and follow the cinder track southwest uphill. It is marked with the red and white stripes of the **GR 11** and a sign indicating 'COLL JOVELL, VALL DEL MADRIU'. You pass a first spring, the **Font de les Ortigues** (**1**) in **2min**. At **5min** the track narrows. Ignore the rough track coming in from the left, and go through a tiny TUNNEL (**2**). At the exit, a signpost indicates a MIRADOR off to the right.

At **10min** the cinder track narrows to a footpath (the CAMÍ DELS MATXOS), to ascend through the Molleres pine wood, and you pass the **Font de les Molleres** (**3**; **15min**). Seven minutes later, there is a large picnic area at the

*Above: Estany d'Engolasters;
right: Sant-Miquel d'Engolasters*

High in the valley of the Riu Madriu

Font dels Corralets (④; **22min**), as well as another signpost indicating the ongoing route. *(The 'Stroll' turns back here.)* Soon you have a lovely view of Sant-Miquel d'Engolasters, as the path climbs more steeply to the **Coll Jovell** (⑤; 1779m/5835ft; **30min**).

Ignore the path to the left (to Tossa del Braibal) and continue on the GR 11 which descends southeast into the idyllic Madriu Valley. At **45min** you JOIN THE **GR 7** FOOTPATH (⑥) coming up from Les Escaldes, turning left (roughly eastwards) along the floor of the **Madriu Valley**, never far from the river.

Now simply amble along the valley, enjoying everything. At **Fontverd** (⑦; 1873m/6143ft; **1h 25min**) there is a refuge and a *font*, and at the **Collet de l'Infern** (1970m/6462ft; **2h**) there is an old refuge. Just beyond lies **La Farga Vella** (⑧; **2h15min**), a flat, open area where iron was worked.

Keep going and you will come to a gorgeous area to just sit and commune with the scenery.

Soon the footpath divides. Ignore the GR 11.6A, which hugs then crosses the river to Collada de la Maiana, instead continuing on the well-trodden **GR 7/GR 11**. The path continues to climb gently along the Madriu Valley, the river curving away to the right before joining the footpath once again at the large, flat pasture known as the **Pla de l'Ingla** (2180m/7150ft; **3h**). At the far end is the **Refugi del Riu dels Orris** (⑨; **3h15min**), a basic shelter sleeping just six people, and the end of our walk. Enjoy your picnic in this beautiful spot, with streams coming down from almost every direction, and the summit of Portelleta to the south.

Return by the same route to the 'CIRCUIT DE LES FONTS' SIGNPOST in around 2h15min (**5h30min**).

Walk 12: MOURGOUILLOU VALLEY AND THE LAKES

Distance: 13km/8mi; 5h30min from the car park (but 7h10min for hikers arriving by train)
Grade: 🔴 moderate as far as the Etang de Comte, but 🔴 difficult thereafter — suitable only for the fit and agile, with some scrambling over boulders. Overall climb and descent of some 780m/2560ft (1180m/3870ft for those arriving by train!) — hard work! GR way-making only as far as the Etang de Comte, cairns thereafter
Equipment: compass/gps, map (such as Randonnées Pyrénéennes Cerdagne-Capcir), strong and waterproof footwear. Much of the walk is at 2000m: see introductory notes on 'Walking', page 38.
Transport: 🚗 (Car tour 4). From Tarascon-sur-Ariège take the N20 south via Ax-les-Thermes and through Mérens-les-Vals; 700 metres beyond the village, where a dual carriageway begins, turn right to the campsite and then follow the forestry track (l'Ubac) that climbs after about 4km/2.5mi up into the Mourgouillou Valley. Park in the car park at the waterfall (42° 38.878'N, 1° 48.812'E). Or 🚆 to Mérens-les-Vals. The line runs from Toulouse to La Tour de Carol (for information contact SNCF: 36 35 within France or ter.sncf.com). To reach the start of the walk from the station, head south along the main road, cross the Ariège River by a stone bridge (4min) and follow the red and white stripes of the GR 10 along the Mourgouillou Valley, climbing to the parking place described above for motorists. (This adds 400m/1h of ascent; allow an extra 40min for the descent.)
For general information: Ax-les-Thermes Tourist Office 05 61 64 60 60, vallees-ax.com
Short walk: Turn round at the **Etang de Comte** (❸; 5km/3mi; 1h40min return; 🔴 an ascent of 300m) or at the **Jasse des Estagnols** (❹; 8.5km/5.3mi; 3h30min return; 🔴 an ascent of 520m).

Black Mérens horses, famous for their possible link with the wild horses of European prehistory, are often seen grazing along the Mourgouillou River valley, the setting for the first part of this walk.

From the CAR PARK by the WATERFALL (⭕) in the **Mourgouillou Valley**, take the forestry track that climbs east, quickly turning right on a steep stone-slabbed path that is marked with the red and white stripes of the **GR 10**. Where the forest opens out to a beautiful plateau, cross the river by the bridge known as the **Pont de Pierre** (❶; **15min**). Beyond the bridge, turn left and continue up the valley by a succession of steep climbs and small plateaux, until you reach a tiny lake, only about 30m/100ft long (**L'Estagnol**; ❷; **45min**). If you are lucky, you may see Mérens horses grazing here.

Just beyond this lake, *leave* the GR10 (which climbs steeply to the right) and continue along the valley to the first big lake, the **Etang de Comte** (❸; **1h**). *(This is an ideal turn-around point for those taking the Short walk.)*

The next section is physically demanding, though not too difficult technically. The ability to use a compass/gps would be a great advantage — *remember that the red and white GR10 flashes are no longer there to help you.*

Pass around Lake Comte, keeping it to your right, and continue climbing along the valley, heading for the pass that you can see ahead. Keep the main stream a little away to your right, and aim also to clip the edge of the birch stand below the pass. (If you have a compass, the bearing is west-southwest.) Some 25 minutes after starting from the tip of the Etang de Comte, the path crosses a small side-stream WATERFALL (**1h25min**), where the water gushes out of a rock. Some 45 minutes beyond the lake, the path swings to the right of a mound and curves towards the main stream (**1h45min**).

Climbing a little further you'll reach the **Jasse des Estagnols** (❹) and a small LAKE (usually dried up), from where you'll see a prominent rocky lump ahead in the middle of the valley — and sheer cliffs to the right, creating a defile that you will enter. After passing the dried-up lake to your right, cross to the opposite bank beyond the lake, using a subtle line of STEPPING STONES. At **2h** cross a side stream and continue on the path which, in another ten minutes, disappears into a pile of rocks. This is just a foretaste of the chaos to come. The way is indicated by CAIRNS and always climbs along the valley, keeping the rocky lump to the left. The exact line may be tortuous, but there is no chance of getting lost, since the steep sides of the valley force you towards the **Etang de Couart** (❺; **3h20min**).

With luck you may see

Etang de Comte

Egyptian vultures here in summer. Standing at the tip of the lake with your back to it (that is, facing east), a valley opens up in front of you, with an obvious path down through it, and steep cliffs to the right. This is the return route.

Head off along the path and come to the **Etang Vidal** (**6**; **3h45min**), passing along the narrow strip between its northern edge and a small but impressive rocky bluff. Continue in the same direction as before. The path is not always clear, but you have only to follow the valley as it descends gradually northeast. Finally, the path swings around northwards and drops rapidly, back to the **Jasse des Estagnols** (**4**; **4h15min**).

From this level plateau, retrace your steps to the CAR PARK by the WATERFALL (**5h30min**).

Walk 13: GORGEOUS GORGES DE LA FRAU

See also photo on pages 18-19
Distance: 14km/8.7mi; 4h15min
Grade: ● easy; a gentle climb of 400m/1315ft at the end of the walk; GR waymarks
Equipment: no special equipment necessary
Transport: 🚗: Car tour 4; park at the entrance to Comus (42° 48.679'N, 1° 53.475'E). Transport is difficult for those who do not have a car; for information about buses and taxis telephone the *gîte d'etape* at Comus 04 68 20 33 69, gites-comus.com or the Ax-les-Thermes Tourist Office 05 61 64 60 60, vallees-ax.com.
Short walk: To save 6km/2h, drive down the white stone track at the southern entrance to Comus and continue some 3km to the obvious START OF THE GORGE (❷), where the track swings up to the left; park here (42° 49.291'N, 1° 51.588'E). Even better: companions willing, arrange to be dropped off at the beginning of the gorge and picked up at the start of the tarmac (D5; ❸) at the other end (see map; 40min, very easy).

On the northern part of the Ariège-Pyrénées, like some 'lost world', the Plateau de Sault is forgotten France. To climb up from Ax-les-Thermes is to go back through centuries, when agriculture was not an industry and birds of prey were not hunted out of the skies. Today, cavers flock here, to the tunnels and gorges that penetrate the plateau. The most stunning of all are the Gorges de la Frau.

Choughs above the Gorges de la Frau and (below): landscape near Comus

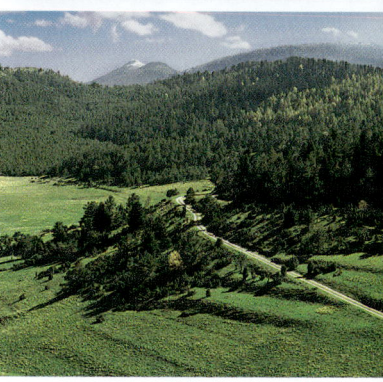

At the southern entrance to the small village of **Comus** you'll see an IRON CROSS (**O**) at the left of a crossroads of tarmac and motorable track (initially sealed). **Start walking** along this track, straight on, below the village. The regular red and white waymarks of the **GR 7** now appear, as well as various waymarkings for the SENTIER CATHARE. After a few minutes, pass a small SEWAGE PLANT (**1**; it passed our sensitive sniff-test as non-noxious). After **15min** come to some low grass-topped cliffs. The track is now descending through fir and beech trees.

After **25min** fork right (the track rising on the left is marked clearly with a red and white cross — 'wrong way'). Keep descending gently, with cliffs rising on each side of you, until the track rises in a tight U-BEND TO THE LEFT (**2**; **50min**) and is marked with a clear red and white 'wrong way' cross. Your path lies over the edge of a slight crest to the right of the bend — in effect carrying straight on into the **Gorges de la Frau**. As you follow the path through fairly dense undergrowth and fallen trees, you immediately feel you've reached real gorge country.

After **1h10min** you'll see before you a SPECTACULAR CLIFF, striped orange and grey with the water streaks of centuries. The awesome scale of the surroundings lends lilliputian dimensions to mere spectators. Hear the electric calls of the jet black *chocards* (choughs), whose favourite home territory you now enter. If you are lucky enough to have the gorge to yourself, you'll discover a wilderness, nothing but trees and weird mountain shapes ... and the echoed buzzing of millions of insects.

Finally the path joins a TARMAC ROAD (**3**; **1h30min**). Follow this quiet and attractive route for as long as you wish, through the dense woodland and strangely-shaped mountains (the setting is shown on pages 18-19). After five minutes (**1h35min**) see, high up on the right, a gathering of NEEDLE-SHARP ROCKS surrounding a central pyramidal peak — a group looking like some sculpted monarch and courtiers.

We chose to walk down the tarmac, through this wilderness of mixed conifer and decidious woodland, for 25 minutes, before TURNING ROUND (**4**; **1h55min**) and starting the long climb back. Anywhere along this road (D5 from Fougax-et-Barrineuf) is ideal for arranging pick-ups, if one of your party agrees to play taxi. Or retrace your steps for a little over 2h, back to **Comus** (**4h15min**).

Walk 14: AMONG THE LAKES

Distance: 13km/8mi; 6h
Grade: ● moderate, with 850m/2800ft of ascent; PR waymarking
Equipment: good quality high-mountain walking equipment — you will reach 2476m/8120ft. See notes on 'Walking', page 38.
Transport: 🚗 From Vicdessos (Car tour 5) take the D8 signposted to Auzat, and continue for 17.7km/11mi to the southernmost end of the Etang (lake) de Soulcem. Beyond a picnic site (11.3km/7mi) the road deteriorates and climbs above the dam wall. Drive beyond the far end of the lake; park just before the 'Aire d'accueil' (42° 39.367'N, 1° 26.919'E); sign: 'Etangs de la Gardelle'.
General information: Tarascon Tourist Office 04 90 91 03 52, lecoeurdelaprovence.fr
Shorter walk: Walk only as far as the Gardelle lakes (**Etangs de la Gardelle**; ❷; 2h), returning the same way (3h20min); the ascent is the same as for the main walk.
Easy walk: ● From the parking, stroll along the path by the **Ruisseau de Soulcem** as far as you like, and return the same way. (The path is known as the '**Chemin des Orris**' for the large number of stone shepherds' huts.)

This is the Ariège at its most awesome. On a warm, sunny day the high-mountain scenery is uplifting, and the lakes, beginning with the Soulcem, can be an inviting shade of blue. But if the weather should deteriorate, be warned that these bare, wind-blasted slopes in the shadow of Montcalm and Estats (the most easterly three-thousanders in the Pyrenees) can become quite vicious.

Begin the walk at the PARKING AREA (⊙): cross the **Ruisseau de Soulcem** by the bridge, following the sign 'ETANGS DE LA GARDELLE'. Beyond the bridge, ignore the clear path to the right; climb the slope in front of you. You will see 'LAC GARDELLE' painted on a rock and the occasional YELLOW FLASH. A clear path gradually emerges; you cross the **Ruisseau de la Gardelle** (**❶**; **30min**) and continue along its left bank.

In **1h30min** reach a pasture where only one of several *orries* (stone shepherds' huts) still stands intact. The path continues along the river to a marshy area, where it swings southeastwards to climb steeply to the first of the Gardelle lakes (**Etangs de la Gardelle**; 2370m/ 7774ft; **❷**; **2h**). A second, smaller lake lies to the southwest, and a third, much larger and extraordinarily round, beyond that. The crests to the west mark the Spanish frontier.

Return to the initial lake, following the marked path to a fourth lake lying to the east, from where the path climbs southeast into a COL marked by a large CAIRN (**❸**; **2h30min**). Once through the col, the Etang de Roumazet is clearly visible below. The path descends to the **Ruisseau de Roumazet** (**❹**; where it is met by another path leading down to the Soulcem plateau, should you wish to shorten

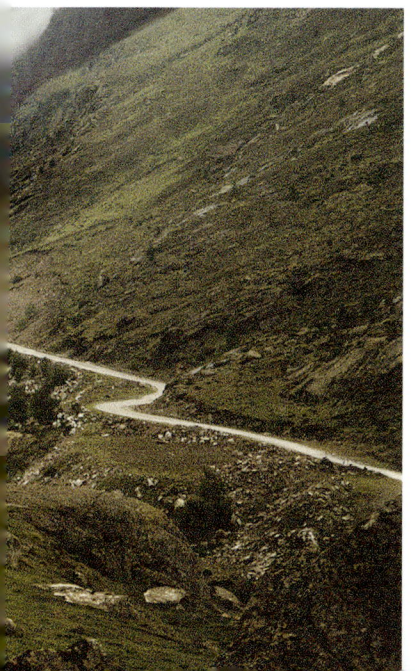

the walk), then swings to the right to the **Etang de Roumazet** (2163m/7095ft; **❺**; **3h15min**).

From the Roumazet lake, the path once again climbs in a southerly direction, and after 45 minutes we are at the final lake, the **Etang de la Soucarrane** (**❻**; **4h**). From the end of this lake the path descends to the **Soulcem Valley**, initially along the outflow of the lake, and then bearing away to descend steeply into the valley bottom. Once on flattish ground again, you may still have energy left to enjoy the many *orries* that line the footpath (**Chemin des Orris**) back to the PARKING AREA (**6h**).

Walk 15: CIRCUIT AROUND LAKE ARTAX (ARTATS)

Distance: 14.4km/9mi; 6h15min
Grade: ● moderate, with 1250m/4100ft of ascent; PR waymarking
Equipment: normal mountain walking equipment; see 'Walking', page 38.
Transport: 🚗 (Car tour 5). From Tarascon-sur-Ariège take the D23, signposted 'Parc Pyrénéen de l'Art Préhistorique'. Continue beyond the Parc to the village of Gourbit. In the village square follow the clear sign 'Etang d'Artax' and continue along a narrow lane to a parking area 'Parking, Randonneurs' 800m/0.5mi from the square (42° 50.222'N, 1° 32.013'E).
General information: Tarascon Tourist Office 04 90 91 03 52, lecoeurdelaprovence.fr
Note: The name of the lake is variously spelt 'Artats' and 'Artax'.
Short walk: ● Walk only as far as the **Etang d'Artax** (❶; 2h) and return the same way (3h20min).
Alternative walk: ● Cut out the Pic de Bassibié and the Pic de Boucarle, by heading straight from the **Etang d'Artax** (❶) to **Pla de Madame** (❹), saving around 1h30min.

The Ariège, with its high mountains and deep valleys, has a reputation as the toughest region in the Pyrenees. This walk shows its gentler face, ideal when low cloud swirls around the frontier peaks.

From the PARKING AREA continue along the lane for 300m, to where it ends south of **Gourbit**. Two paths lead off from this point. One is signposted 'Col de Lastris' and is the way you will be returning at the end of the day. **Start the walk** by following the route to the right, marked 'L'ETANG D'ARTAX' (○), a truly delightful stone-slabbed footpath climbing southwestwards through beech woods. Various other paths and tracks cross the route, but you will not go wrong as long as you follow the YELLOW PAINT flashes (while remembering not to enter any paths marked with a yellow 'X').

Eventually you reach the northeast corner of the **Etang d'Artax** (1695m/5560ft; ❶; 2h), where there are two little cabins. This is a kinder, softer Ariège than you'll experience on Walk 14, the lake nestling in the palm of grassy slopes. The big mound to the west is Pic de Bassibié, the next goal. (*But for the Alternative walk, strike out along the eastern shore of the lake and climb southeast directly to Pla de Madame.*)

To continue the main walk, take the little path that climbs northwards from behind the CABINS and, once on top of the ridge, simply head southwest to the **Pic de Bassibié** (2114m/6934ft; ❷; 3h30min). From the top of this easy dome there are stupendous

Lake Artax

views west towards Mont Valier and east towards Carlit.

The itinerary now describes a semicircle along the southern crests that look down on the lake. Just stroll through the grass, past the **Pic de Boucarle** (❸) to **Pla de Madame** (*where the Alternative walk joins the ridge;* ❹; **4h15min**). Now continue to **Roc de Querquéou** (1840m/6035ft; ❺), where the ridge — the **Crête du Courral Terrous** — swings northeast and descends gently to the **Col de Lastris** (1427m/4680ft; ❻; **5h15min**).

At the col, a clear sign 'GOURBIT', indicates the way back to the PARKING AREA south of **Gourbit** (**6h15min**).

Walk 16: CRÊTE DES ISARDS

Distance: 11.5km/7.2mi; 7h
Grade: ● moderate, with about 850m/2790ft of ascent; PR and GR waymarking
Equipment: mountain walking equipment according to season (highest point 2381m/7810ft); see notes on 'Walking', page 38. The Riutort Valley can be quite boggy: wear stout, water-resistant footwear.
Transport: 🚗 (Car tour 5). From Tarascon-sur-Ariège take the N20 south to Les Cabannes. Turn into the village and follow signs for Aston and Barrage de Laparan (D520A). The road gradually deteriorates but is quite passable. Park after 20km, just beyond the dam wall, beside the little Riutort waterfall (42° 40.369'N, 1° 42.525'E).
General information: Tarascon Tourist Office 04 90 91 03 52, lecoeurdelaprovence.fr
Note: The modern and comfortable Refuge du Rulhe (05 61 65 65 01, end May-end Sept, rulhe.com), the farthest point of the walk, is an excellent base for treks.
Shorter walk: ● From the **Cabane de Rieutort** (**❶**) go directly to the **Refuge du Rulhe** (**❻**) along the Riutort Valley, saving 1h30min. The path is GR-marked (allow 3h out and 2h30min by the same route).
Easy walk: ● From the parking area (**○**), amble beside the **Etang de Laparan** and as far along the valley as you wish.

The climax of this itinerary, the Crête des Isards, provides an exciting but safe ridge walk with marvellous views. Given the vertiginous drops on each side, you'll understand how it got its name.

Start out from the PARKING AREA at the **Riutort** WATERFALL (**○**), following the clear path signposted 'REFUGE DU RULHE' and marked with yellow flashes. The rocky path climbs very steeply at first, but after about **20min** of hard effort, you enter the pastures and follow the valley as it curves around towards the south.

At the **Cabane du Riutort** (1825m/5986ft; **❶**; **1h15min**), we leave the Riutort Valley footpath *(unless following the Alternative walk above)*. Do not cross the river by the bridge, but, instead, attack the slope to the east. This is not a marked path, but the open hillside, though steep, presents no problems. About half-way up, swing more to the north and in just under an hour reach the **Col de la Didorte** (2093m/6865ft; **❷**; **2h10min**).

From here you will follow the **GR 10**, marked by red and white stripes, climbing southeast at first, and then swinging south as you make your way all along the ridge as far as the Col de Belh. The terrain is increasing spectacular, and onwards from the highest point (**Pic de Belh**, 2381m/7810ft; **❸**) the ridge is very aptly known as the **Crête des Isards**, a reference to the agile Pyrenean chamois. The ridge ends at the **Col de Belh** (2247m/7370ft; **❹**; **4h**). Do not take the path northeast here; instead take the path southwest to the **Col de Terre Negre** (**❺**) and on down to the **Refuge du Rulhe** (2185m/7167ft; **❻**; **4h30min**), a large, modern refuge built on a wide grassy shelf high above the **Ruisseau de l'Estagnol**.

After refreshments, take the path clearly marked with red and white stripes (a variation of the GR10) along the **Riutort Valley** back to the **Cabane du Riutort** (**❶**; **5h45min**), and then retrace your steps to the **Riutort** WATERFALL PARKING (**7h**).

Walk 16: Crête des Isards   87

Fingerposts on the GR 10 indicating the Refuge de Rulhe and the Etang de Laparan

Walk 17: PARC NACIONAL D'AIGÜESTORTES

Distance: 10km/6.2mi; 3h50min *from the Estany de Sant Maurici*
Grade: ● moderate, with a climb of 350m/1150ft; well signposted
Equipment: mountain walking equipment according to season — see notes on 'Walking', page 38.
Transport: 🚗 (Car tour 6). Park at Prat de Pierró (42° 35.084'N, 1° 2.881'E); in winter phone the park office to ask if the car park is open (it often closes from 1/12 to Easter); in high summer ask if there is space. Take a jeep-taxi to the lake and back. If you decide to walk (on a well-signposted path) allow an extra 250m/820ft of ascent (1h15min up, 45min down).
General information: Vielha Tourist Office 973 64 06 88, visitvaldaran.com; Parc Nacional d'Aigüestortes 973 69 61 89, parcs naturals.gencat.cat/en/xarxa-de-parcs/aiguestortes/inici. Jeep/taxis: 629 205 489, taxisvalldeboi.com
Alternative walk: ●❗ For the very fit! Continue to ascend from the Estanys de Monestero to the summit. Climb (with difficulty) a steeply zigzagging path to **Coll de Monestero** (ⓐ) and then head right, keeping the top of the summit ridge to your right (terrific views). The final, cairn-marked section to the **Pic de Peguera** (ⓑ), is only recommended for very experienced mountain walkers. Add 4km/2.5mi; 750m/2460ft of ascent (3h20min) there and back from the Estanys.

Aigüestortes, literally translated, means 'twisted waters'. But the beautiful marshes, streams, waterfalls and lakes of the Parc Nacional d'Aigüestortes i Estany de Sant Maurici have proved to be a curse. The waters are no longer free and rushing, but 'straightened out' — for hydroelectricity projects. One of only two national parks in the Spanish Pyrenees, the international status of Aigüestortes with its 50 lakes is threatened. Our walk takes you to a part of the park that has almost escaped being tamed.

Alight from the jeep-taxi at **Estany** (lake) **de Sant Maurici**. The lake is beautiful when full, but bear in mind that the level can drop. **Start out** by heading south on the path that skirts the wall of the dam; it's signed 'REFUGIO ERNEST MALLAFRE' (○). When it divides, take the left-hand, lower route. Descend to a flat BRIDGE and pass the REFUGE (❶; 15min). The path (now signposted 'MONESTERO') zigzags steeply uphill, through flowers and thistles covered with butterflies, for which the park is well known.

At **35min** start climbing through firs, with an attractive stream on the left. Boardwalks protect the marshy ground from erosion. Eventually a vast rocky lump materialises ahead, and you keep it to your left, to follow the valley of **Monestero**, not Seca.

Soon the 'lump' is directly on your left and you arrive at a large plateau ringed by mountains — the **Prat de Monestero** (❷; 1h). Now a stream lies left, and you pass little **Lake Feixant** and the larger **Estany Baix de Monestero** (❸; 1h15min).

Beyond this lake the path is no longer as well marked, but there are some small CAIRNS. You climb steeply to another grassy pasture by the **Estanys de Monestero** (❹; 2h10min). Here the Pic de Peguera is straight ahead — at 2982m/9780ft, the highest peak in this part of the park. It's slightly to the right of Monestero (2878m/ 9440ft), with the Coll de Monestero in between. This is a perfect picnic spot and base for the more demanding climb facing those doing the Alternative walk.

Retrace your steps to the **Estany de Sant Maurici** (3h50min).

From Lake Sant Maurici there's an iconic view of 'Els Encantats' ('The Enchanted') — twin granite peaks, said to represent shepherds turned to stone for not honouring Sant Maurici.

Walk 18: A TASTE OF THE THE BARONNIES

Distance: 5.3km/3.3mi; 2h20min
Grade: ● easy climb of 250m/820ft; fairly steep descent at the end; well waymarked with blue and yellow 'wolf' motifs (Sentier du Pacte des Loups) .
Equipment: rubber boots advisable, otherwise no special equipment — but see introductory notes on 'Walking', page 38.
Transport: 🚗 (Car tour 7 to Esparros). Esparros best accessed by car, but there may also be an infrequent minibus service. For all information, contact the Tourist Office La-Barthe-de-Neste 05 62 98 87 02, coeurdespyrenees.com/en/heart-of-the-pyrenees. From Esparros, drive downhill towards Laborde, and immediately after passing the *mairie* take the first left (south). After about 1.5km/1mi, you come to a tight U-bend and narrow track on your left with a yellow sign for 'Cascade': park across the road for the Short walk (43° 1.184'N, 0° 19.289'E). For the main walk, continue along the road. At 4.5km/2.8mi from the village the tarmac ends at a barrier, which is normally open. (If it should be closed, park as nearby as possible and continue on foot, adding 2.5km/1.5mi each way.) Beyond the barrier continue on good track and take the right fork just beyond the animal marshalling corral. You come to an exposed plateau at a crossroads of four tracks, the Col de Couradabat: park here (43° 0.489'N, 0° 18.433'E).

Short walk (possible in dry weather only): Park by the tight U-bend (❹; see above) and follow signs for 'CASCADE'. ● You'll walk past flower-filled meadows (shown below) and reach an impressive moss-clothed WATERFALL (❺; 40min return). *The path can get very boggy and may be closed during wet spells.*

Alternative walk: To avoid the fairly steep descent from the **Col des Estrets** (❶; the pass reached in 1h10min), return along your outgoing route (●; 2h20min). But first climb the RIDGE and enjoy the view of the astonishingly remote country of these 'hidden' Baronnies valleys.

Below and opposite: in the Baronnies

Walk 18: A taste of the Baronnies

The Baronnies is an abandoned area, returning to nature — neither flat enough for modern agriculture, nor high enough for ski development. And what nature! We have seen *chevreuil* (roe deer), *sanglier* (wild boar) and *vautour fauves* (griffon vultures) in a single outing; the streams are believed to be home to one of the most elusive creatures of the Pyrenees, the *desman*, the aquatic mole-like animal with a trumpet-shaped nose shown here. We haven't seen it — but you might.

Start the walk from the crossroads of tracks at the **Col de Couradabat** (⊙), where you should take the left-hand route (south) past a little stone *cabane* — often still used by shepherds and workers from the nearby mine. Ignoring a path to the left at the *cabane*, keep to the track as it climbs through beech wood. As you near the top of the climb, you can hope to see vultures — we once did. That same day we also met up with an old *berger* (shepherd), who told us he had been camping out and watching his sheep for a week. He presented a marvellous example of travelling light — all he appeared to have in his tiny rucksack was a half-drunk bottle of wine!

The track makes for a low pass in the ridge. Ignore the divide which curves to the right and continue climbing ahead into the PASS (**Col des Estrets**; ❶; 1h10min). Pause at the top, to look behind you for one of the most spectacular views you'll ever have of the more remote corners in the Pyrenees. *'Sauvage'*, say the French, to describe such a wilderness.

Ignoring the forestry track which continues ahead, pick up your ongoing

Visit the ancient abbey of Escaladieu on your way to Esparros (Car tour 7)

92 Landscapes of the Pyrenees

footpath on the far side of the pass by bearing left (north). The path soon heads eastwards once more. It gradually rises up through box and pine (quite a few of the huge old pines are wreathed in lichen) to reach the TOP OF A RIDGE (**1h20min**). From here there are splendid views north to Esparros, and agricultural plains fill in the backdrop as far as the eye can see.

Continue eastwards along the ridge, keeping a plantation fence to your left. At the **Col des Arès** (❷; **1h30min**), abandon the ridge and take a left turn between this plantation and another; the blue/yellow 'wolf' motifs guide you. Your path descends steeply between the plantations and then into a dense forest of beech. At **1h40min** emerge from the beech into another fir plantation. Running through here, the path narrows, then joins the MAIN TRACK FROM ESPARROS (❸; **1h55min**).

Turn left to ascend back to the crossroads at the **Col de Couradabat** (**2h20min**).

Left, below: in the Baronnies

Walk 19: THE ROOF OF THE PYRENEES

Distance: 6km/3.7mi; 5h
Grade: ● moderate — 1059m/3475ft of quite demanding ascent; PR and local waymarking
Equipment: mountain walking equipment according to season — see introductory notes on 'Walking', page 38. The final col (Port de Venasque), at 2444m/8018ft, is likely to be in snow from November till late spring.
Transport: 🚗 (Car tour 7). From Luchon continue south on the D125 for 5km and then take the left turn to the Hospice de France, where there is a large car park (42° 43.284'N, 0° 39.218'E).
For general information: telephone the Luchon Tourist Office 05 61 79 21 21, pyrenees31.com/en
Shorter walk: Go only as far as the **Refuge de Venasque** (**5**); 30 places, staffed May to October (refugedevenasque.ffcam.fr; tel. 06 89 49 82 27 or 09 87 88 14 69) for a drink and a meal, then return the same way: ● an ascent of about 850m/2800ft; 4h15min return.
Alternative walk: ● From the Port de Venasque, the seriously fit can easily ascend to the summit of **Pic de Sauvegarde** (2738m/8980ft; **8**) — the mountain to the west of the pass) by the clear path which heads off to the right, from just below the pass on the Spanish side of the border. Allow 2h for the round trip from the pass (making 7h in total).

A neto (3404m/11,165ft), in Spain, is the highest peak in the Pyrenees. An ascent is outside the scope of this book, but the classic approach from the Hospice de France, near Luchon, to the Port de Venasque, on the Franco-Spanish frontier, makes a memorable day out in the historic footsteps of many of the great 'Pyreneists'.

Looking back towards the Hospice de France on the ascent to the border with Spain (the Port de Venasque)

Start out at the CAR PARK (**0**) by the **Hospice de France**, built by the Knights of St John of Jerusalem. Walk to the front of the building, then turn right, following the sign 'PORT DE VENASQUE'. Cross the stream and follow the clear path through pasture and woodland, heading into a narrow valley and climbing a little west of south. After **14min** cross the stream on a concrete and metal BRIDGE (**1**). The path begins to zigzag up more steeply, and the valley closes in, allowing no possibility of getting lost.

When you arrive at the foot of a huge escarpment, cross the STREAM ON STEPPING STONES (**2**; **1h**) below the waterfall and continue up the grassy slope to the left of the rock face. At **1h25min** cross two small streams. Twenty minutes later the PATH HEADS WEST (**3**; **1h45min**) and sweeps across to the centre of the valley, taking you above the escarpment. As you zigzag up, the views back are increasingly awesome. The Hospice de France is now only a dot in a green clearing, with the slopes of the Montagut range behind it, rising up through forest to bare summits.

At **2h03min** you reach a crest and enter the upper valley. Your thighs can relax a bit. The refuge just beyond the crest is a ruin, but the Refuge de Venasque, where you are heading, is now only an easy 25 minutes away. Take the RIGHT-HAND FORK at **2h12min** (**4**). When you finally reach the **Refuge de Venasque** (**5**; **2h30min**), you will no doubt agree that its lakeside setting, beside the beautiful **Boums du Port** (**6**), is postcard-perfect. Two other, smaller lakes lie close by. *(The Shorter walk returns from here.)*

For the main walk, continue along the path to the east (without crossing the stream). After passing around a small rise, resume your southerly trajectory: the lake will be on your right and cliffs to your left. The path steepens on the northwest face of the **Pic de la Mine**, then enters a scree-strewn gully wedged between that mountain and the Pic de Sauvegarde to your right.

After 30 minutes of climbing from the refuge, a narrow pass suddenly opens in front of you. One more step through the **Port de Venasque** (2444m/8016ft; **7**; **3h**) and you are in Spain. Savour the moment. Steeply below your feet lies the upper Esera Valley and beyond it the powerful Maladeta Massif, crowned by the Pico de Aneto.

Aneto was not conquered until 1842 (by a team led by the Russian climber, Platon de Tchihatcheff). The early explorers headed down into the Esera Valley before beginning the assault on the roof of the Pyrenees. You, however, will be returning by the same route to the **Hospice de France** (**5h**).

Walk 20: CIRQUE DE GAVARNIE

Distance: 9km/5.6mi; 3h
Grade: ● an easy climb of 400m/1315ft — but the second part of the walk is dangerous if there is snow, in which case you should simply retrace your steps from the *cirque*, rather than continue.
Equipment: no special equipment, but see introductory notes on 'Walking', page 38.
Transport: 🚌 mid-June to mid-September, lio-occitanie.fr, tel: 08 06 80 03 50 from Tarbes or Lourdes; or 🚗: Car tour 8; obligatory parking in the car park at the entrance to Gavarnie village (42° 44.114'N, 0° 0.667'E).
General information: Gavarnie Tourist Office 05 62 92 49 10, gavarnie.com
Short walk: After reaching the **Hotel du Cirque** (❸), return to Gavarnie by the same route (7.4km/4.6mi; 2h10min; ● easy climb, as above).

96 Landscapes of the Pyrenees

Gavarnie is a very popular climbing and walking centre in the Pyrenees and its *cirque* is one of the great spectacles of the world. If you're in the area on no account miss this — but, since it attracts more than half a million visitors a year, *do* avoid weekends. The glacier-scoured wall of rock, rising more than 1300m/4265ft from the valley floor and with a circumference of over 3km/2mi, is visible from some distance. As you approach the village, watch out, too, for the famous Brèche de Roland (photo on pages 100-101), the gap in the top of this rock wall. According to legend, the *brèche* was smashed out of the rock by the dying Roland, commander of Charlemagne's rearguard (see Walks 28 and 29).

Starting out from the centre of **Gavarnie** (○), take the same route as the *muletiers,* and head south towards the *cirque.* (If you prefer, you can take the pony-ride.) After **5min** cross the **Pont Brioule** (❶) by the Bergerie Café. The tarmac road soon becomes track, and you continue along the 'rive droite'.

After **10min**, just before a MODERN BARN (❷), pass a path to the left, signposted 'Espuguettes' (among others) — this is the way you will be returning later in the day. For now, continue beside the river, the **Gave de Gavarnie**, which

Walk 20: Cirque de Gavarnie

has its source high up in the glaciers of the *cirque*.

The track soon rises steeply until, after **20min**, you top the crest of a hill for your first view of the beautiful **La Prade** plateau. You are now within the Parc National des Pyrénées which links up, at the top of the *cirque*, with the Ordesa National Park in Spain (Walk 26).

Beyond the plateau the track rises up through the trees to a narrow gorge, at the end of which the **Hotel du Cirque** (❸; **1h05min**) sits just out of reach of the midday shadow. Once the hotel hosted the 'greats' — from Russell (see Walk 21) and Charles Packe, to Gavarnie's last high-mountain guide, George Adagas. Nowadays, sadly, it is open only for refreshments and souvenirs.

This is as far as the ponies go but, if you wish, you may continue to the foot of the **Cirque de Gavarnie** itself and cool off in the spray of the Grande Cascade (ⓐ; allow 1h30min extra for this ascent of 350m/1150ft and retracing steps).

The return to Gavarnie may be by the same route (Short walk), but a more interesting alternative is to take the path that climbs up through the Bois d'Arribama, a wood offering welcome shade on a hot day.

From in front of the Hotel du Cirque follow the sign 'GAVARNIE PAR LES ESPUGUES' and ascend northwards on a narrow path that passes along the side of the hotel. In five minutes (**1h10min**) you mount a small crest, from where there are good views back to Gavarnie. After another five minutes the path passes under high cliffs and at one point over an avalanche slope. (If there is snow, this section is *dangerous*, so take local advice before setting off on this part of the walk.)

After a little over **2h** you reach a HUT (❹), the **Refuge du Pailha** (open only in Jul/Aug, refugedupailha.com). From here there are views of the twin peaks, Petit and Grand Astazou, and the Couloir Swan separating them (southeast), Pailla Rouge (the 'red rock', east), and Pimené directly ahead (northeast).

After some **2h10min** cross a bridge to emerge on the **Plateau de Pailla** (❺), a superb vantage point and picnic area. From the plateau the path descends northwest and then zigzags towards Gavarnie, rejoining the original path at the BARN (❷) ten minutes from the Bergerie Café. Turn right to the centre of **Gavarnie** (**3h**).

Cirque de Gavarnie

Walk 21: RUSSELL'S CAVES

See also photo on pages 26-27
Distance: 9.6km/6mi; 4h30min
Grade: 🔴 moderate — involves a strenuous ascent of some 750m/2460ft (up to 2500m/8200ft), and possibly the crossing of permanent snow
Equipment: Study the introductory notes on high-mountain walking (page 38): in early or late season crampons, ice-axe and gaiters may be required. Water is plentiful.
Transport: 🚖 taxi (from the Café Glaciers in Gavarnie, telephone 05 62 92 47 30) or 🚗 to the Barrage (dam) d'Ossoue (Car tour 8). Take the road out of Gavarnie towards the ski station and, at the first hairpin bend, follow the 'Ossoue' sign). The first 4km are on tarmac, the remaining 3km on track; pre-arrange with the taxi driver for your return. Or on foot from Gavarnie to the dam (only for the *ultra*-fit)!
Useful contact: Gavarnie Tourist Office 05 62 92 49 10, gavarnie.com
Short walk: Follow the main walk to the top of the FIRST CASCADE (❷), then retrace your steps (4.3km/2.7mi; 2h return; 🔵 easy climb of 200m/650ft).
Alternative walks: 🔴 Fit walkers may wish to continue along the path from Russell's caves for a further three-quarters of an hour to the **Refuge de Bayssellance** (ⓐ), the highest point on the GR 10 footpath (staffed mid-June to mid-September; check by phoning 09 74 77 66 52 or 06 88 29 89 60, refuge.bayssellance.ffcam.fr). Another possibility is to get closer to the **Glacier d'Ossoue** (ⓑ) by taking the CAIRNED PATH ● on the left, beginning about 200m past the caves and climbing along the base of **Petit Vignemale**. *It is not advisable to walk on the glacier without rope and crampons and the knowledge of how to use them.*

Count Henry Patrick Marie Russell-Killough (1834-1909) was one of the great traveller-eccentrics. His early explorations took him all over the world, but such became his obsession with the Pyrenees, and especially Vignemale (3298m/10,820ft), that he had a series of caves cut into the mountain where he lived and entertained for part of the year. The most accessible are the Grottes Bellevue, near the largest glacier in the Pyrenees.

Looking south across the Barrage d'Ossoue

Starting from the end of the track along the **Ossoue Valley**, take the **HRP** PATH (❍) that keeps the **Barrage d'Ossoue** to the left. Beyond the lake the path continues to a concrete bridge over the **Oulettes d'Ossoue** (❶; **35min**) and then zigzags up to the top of a FIRST CASCADE (❷; **1h**), after which it descends towards the stream (and an attractive picnic spot). *(The Short walk turns back here.)*

After **1h30min** you will reach the place known as the '**Pont de Neige**' (❸; snow bridge) where, in the past, there was always permanent *névé* (porous ice formed from old snow). When we wrote the first edition of this book it was always at least 30 paces across but, due to climate warming, there was no snow at all in August 2020. However, always exercise great care here, especially in spring and autumn, when the snow may be extensive.

After **1h55min** the path tops a rise, and you'll see to your left the CASCADE that is fed by the Ossoue Glacier, the largest glacier remaining in the Pyrenees. Behind you there is a magnificent view of the frontier peaks and the Brèche de Roland (Walk 22). Crossing the stream below the cascade (on stones) you may wish to collect water.

From the stream climb in steep zigzags until you come to a wall of rock protruding from the scree. Cut into it are **Russell's Caves** —the **Grottes Bellevue** (❹; **2h 50min**). And what a view! — to the west the foot of the Ossoue Glacier, to the south the massif of Monte Perdido, the Brèche de Roland and Taillon. Russell's own cave, with a stone sleeping platform, is high enough to stand up in. Stay a while to contemplate the passion of this extraordinary man and the scene, a century ago, when he entertained society friends on his 'estate'.

Returning by the same route, you will be back at the **Barrage d'Ossoue** in just under 2h (**4h30min**).

Walk 22: BRECHE DE ROLAND

Distance: 11.2km/7mi; 6h
Grade: ● difficult — involves a climb of some 500m/1640ft. The description below is of summer conditions (mid-July to end August); the rest of the year this route is suitable only for mountaineers and ski-mountaineers with proper equipment and skills.
Equipment: mountain walking equipment appropriate to the season — see introductory notes on 'Walking', page 38.
Transport: 🚖 taxi (from the Café Glaciers in Gavarnie, telephone 05 62 92 47 30) or 🚗 (Car tour 8) to the Col de Tentes (42° 42.663'N, 0° 2.695'E) on the road past the ski station. Arrange a taxi for the return.
Useful contacts: Gavarnie Tourist Office 05 62 92 49 10, gavarnie.com; Refuge Sarradets/Refuge de la Brèche de Roland 06 83 38 13 24, refugebrechederoland.ffcam.fr (staffed from 1st June to 30th September approximately)
Short walks: Go as far as the Refuge des Sarradets (④) for a magnificent view of the *brèche*, then retrace your steps (4h; ● easy climb of 300m/985ft). Or, from the parking at the Col de Tentes, take the path eastwards that leads first to **Pic de Tentes** (2322m/7616ft; ⓐ) and then the **Pic de la Pahule** (2292m/7518ft; (ⓑ), for some of the most impressive panoramas you will ever witness. ● An easy 2h there and back.
Alternative walk: The ultra-fit can continue through the *brèche* to the summit of the **Pic du Taillon** (3144m/10,312ft; ⓒ) and thus 'bag' an easy three-thousander. Once through the *brèche*, take the clear path to the right (westwards), first of all under the walls of the **Pic Bazillac**, past the 'finger' of the so-called *fausse* (false) *brèche*, and then along the ridge. ● The ascent poses no problems except snow, but will add 2h30min to your times — the views are well worth it if you have the energy.

A classic walk of the Central Pyrenees, this hike takes you to a gap in the wall of rock that forms a natural frontier between France and Spain. Legend insists that this curious breach in solid rock was caused by a blow from Durandel, the indestructable sword thrown by Roland when he was mortally wounded by his Saracen foe at Roncesvalles (see Walk 29).

Our timings start from the CAR PARK (〇) at the **Col de Tentes**. Follow the remains of an ice-fissured tarmac road southwestwards. This peters out into a rough path, high above the **Pouey Aspé Valley**, and after 2km/1.25mi you reach the frontier pass known to some as the **Port de Gavarnie**, and to others as the **Puerto de Boucharo** (❶; **30min**). Do not go through the pass. Instead, take the steep path heading back eastwards along the opposite rim of the Pouey Aspé.

Brèche de Roland

Pass a 'PARC NATIONAL' sign warning you of the dangers of high-altitude mountain walking. And indeed, this is an area fraught with avalanches, stone-falls and, because of the high altitude, sudden weather changes. But the path is clear, and *on a fine day this is an expedition well within the reach of most fit walkers.* The sharp ascent ends after about **36min** at a huge BOULDER-STREWN PLATEAU under the north face of **Taillon**, a mountain much loved by climbers. The **Glacier des Gabiétous** is visible to the right.

After **1h30min** draw level with the far end of Taillon, where the path begins to rise sharply to the right. You eventually come to SIGNPOSTS (❷; **1h50min**) with an arrow pointing down to Gavarnie by the route you would have travelled had you walked up from the village. Arrows also show the route to the ('Refuge de la Brèche de Roland' but are surplus to requirements, as the waymarked path is clear, ascending a wide gully, sometimes running with water and sometimes CHAINS to help you on the more difficult sections.

After **2h** you see ahead the strange MONOLITHIC ROCK known as the *'fausse* (false) *brèche'*. Closer to the path are some strangely striated cliffs, giving a foretaste of the landscape in the canyons of the Spanish Ordesa (Walk 26). Climb for five minutes more (**2h05min**) and pass the **Glacier du Taillon**, quite close on your right.

The **Col des Sarradets** (❸; **2h35min**) gives you your first view of the refuge and your first close-up of the amazing Brèche de Roland. When you reach the **Refuge des Sarradets** (❹; **2h40min**) have a rest, buy some refreshments (or indeed stay the night — reservation *essential* at peak times) and enjoy the most stupendous views of the Cirque de Gavarnie.

Then follow a faint path climbing the spine of a vast SCREE-SLOPE, to reach a plateau below the *brèche* (**3h10min**). You are at the foot of what was once the **Glacier de la Brèche**. In high summer the way up should be snow-free. Earlier or later it will be more difficult. However you'll be in the company of many other people, of all ages and abilities, some leaping up with the help of crampons and ice axes, others picking their way gingerly over patches of less slippery snow.

The **Brèche de Roland** (❺; **3h 30min**) opens up one of the world's great views. In clear weather you can see rank after rank of the differently-coloured rock walls of Spain's famous canyons. Sunset here is magical. Step through and you're in Spain.

Return by the same route to the **Col de Tentes** (**6h**).

Sharing the trail with some mules, just before the Refuge Wallon (Walk 23)

Walk 23: CIRCUIT FROM THE PONT D'ESPAGNE VIA THE VALLEE DU MARCADAU AND LAC DU POURTET

Distance: 18.7km/11.6mi; 6h45min
Note: If you wish to eat at the Refuge Wallon or the Hôtellerie du Lac de Gaube it's best to make a reservation. Always carry refreshments with you!
Grade: ● moderate, with a climb of 950m/3115ft; well signposted
Equipment: stout shoes; see also notes on 'Walking', page 38.
Transport: 🚕 taxi (from Cauterets, telephone 06 14 25 58 20 mobile) or 🚗 (Car tour 8) to the Pont d'Espagne (42° 51.113'N, 0° 8.174'W). Pre-arrange a taxi for the return.
Useful contacts: Cauterets Tourist Office 05 62 92 50 50, cauterets.com; Refuge Wallon (staffed from early Feb to end Sep) 09 88 77 37 90, refuge-marcadau.csvss.fr/en/home
Short walk: Go as far as you like along the Vallée du Marcadau and retrace steps — to the **Refuge Wallon Marcadau** (❸) and back will take about 3h30min (14.4km/8.9mi, ● an easy climb of some 300m/985ft).
Alternative walk: From Pont d'Espagne the **GR 10** footpath ascends the right bank of the river to the **Lac de Gaube** — ● an easy, lovely walk (just over 200m/650ft of ascent; 2h return). In summer, refreshments are available at **l'Hôtellerie du Lac de Gaube** (ⓐ; 06 74 51 56 28). Return the same way or take the track via the chair lift (just 20min down from the lake) — or perhaps ride down!

The Marcadau is one of those rare Pyrenean valleys that has something of the ambiance of the 'Grand Nord'. It leads to the Refuge Wallon Marcadau, with its feeling of high-mountain isolation, and from there the route climbs steeply to the lakes of Nère and Pourtet, before descending again towards Pont d'Espagne.

Start out at **Pont d'Espagne** (1460m/4789ft; **⓿**) and take the road to the **Chalet Refuge du Clot** (**❶**). Cross two bridges over the **Gave du Marcadau** and turn right on a tarmac road (closed to traffic), following signs to 'MARCADAU'. The road takes you westwards through a forest of silver fir until, after **45min**, you round a corner to see the open floor of the **Vallée du Marcadau** surrounded by high peaks, the stream sparkling in the sunshine. The road now becomes a jeep track and makes for the head of the valley, keeping the stream to the right.

After **1h** reach a collection of signs and turn left for 'VALLÉE DU MARCADAU/REFUGE WALLON'. The jeep track ascends through woodland, at **1h25min** emerging into an open area in the upper valley, where there are pleasant picnic spots beside the stream. Cross the stream on the **Pont d'Estalounque** (**❷**) and then continue along the opposite bank, after ten minutes climbing steeply through firs and

104

then Scots pine. A small PLATEAU (**1h50min**) gives you some magnificent views along the river, which is now far below.

After **2h05min** come to 'PARC NATIONAL' signs. Ignore the left turn over the bridge (towards the Col d'Arratille) and continue on, to reach the **Refuge Wallon Marcadau** in five minutes more (**❸**; **2h10min**). Standing at 1866m/ 6120ft, this is one of the more substantial refuges, with refreshment, meals, and accommodation; it closes at the end of September, only the petit refuge for mountaineers then remaining open. *(The Short walk turns back here.)*

To continue on the main itinerary, follow the sign 'LAC NÈRE, LAC DU POURTET', passing a CHAPEL (**❹**) on your left. Cairns mark the clear path which climbs northwest, cutting between ancient pines, their massive roots ready to trip up the unwary. Follow the path to the right and, at **2h25min**, you begin to zigzag steeply up through a maze of water- and animal-eroded paths. The official path is marked with the occasional CAIRN, but any route to the top will do.

After less than ten minutes (**2h35min**) use STEPPING STONES to cross a vigorous stream (don't miss an opportunity to fill water bottles here) and follow the path for another 20 minutes, when another obvious stepping-stone STREAM CROSSING will present itself on the left (**5**; **2h55min**). Do *not*, however, be tempted to take this HRP path, as you should keep the stream on your *left*. Look ahead and see your path zigzagging up the hillside.

You come to a GRASSY PLATEAU, then start to climb quite steeply again. At this point look behind for fantastic views of Vignemale (see Walk 21). The path levels out at **3h**, but after a short while the hard work starts again for another 10-minute climb to another GRASSY PLATEAU (**3h10min**).

Still keeping the stream on the left, walk across this plateau towards the mountains ahead. You're wondering how any path can manage to scale such steep cliffs. Worry not: as is often the way with footpaths, this one picks a perfectly manageable route, and the well-cairned path zigzags up, to deposit surprised walkers at the edge of the idyllic rock-ringed mountaintop **Lac Nère** (**6**; **3h45min**).

The path rises quite quickly from the right-hand side of the lake, continuing northwards, leaving the bowl at its far end. Note the cairns (there may also be occasional red waymarking) — though the path is quite clear. After some 10 minutes' climbing (**3h55min**), come to a moonscape of loose rocks ringed by mountains. In the company of your own echo, pick your way straight ahead over rocks, following cairns and perhaps more splodges of red paint, to climb to a second lake — the **Lac du Pourtet** (**7**; **4h15min**).

Follow the path along the right-hand side of the lake, until it turns right (east). Do not be tempted to walk to the tip of the lake. Your path comes to a ridge and then starts its long, long descent — rather steeply at first — over slippery rubble, to the first of several LOWER LAKES (**4h30min**). The tree-covered slopes of the Vallée du Marcadau, your goal, come into view. Watch out for fleet-footed izard (Pyrenean chamois) here.

At **4h50min** come over another rise and take the lower of two paths offered, running beside the **Ruisseau du Pourtet**. At **5h** come to and pass another TWO LAKES in quick succession, after about eight minutes curving north to enter a new valley.

At **5h20min** the path begins to zigzag, crossing a stream and a boulder-strewn area. When it recrosses the stream and almost immediately divides, take the RIGHT-HAND FORK (**8**; **5h35min**; to the left there is a viewpoint), descending through increasingly dense woodland until, you reach the bottom, regaining your original route by crossing the **Pont du Cayan** (**9**; **5h35min**). Turn left and retrace the first section of the walk back to **Pont d'Espagne** (**6h45min**).

Walk 24: VALLE DE PINETA AND PUNTA DEL VALLE

Distance: 9.4km/5.8mi; 7h30min
Grade: ● very strenuous ascent of 1200m/3940ft, but not technically difficult; GR waymarking.
Important: The full walk involves ascending to 2460m/8070ft, which means that there will be snow on the upper section between late October and late June. Do not flirt with steep snow slopes without proper equipment and experience; be content to turn around at the snow line and make a safe descent.
Equipment: proper mountain walking equipment, appropriate to the season — see introductory notes on 'Walking', page 38.
Transport: 🚗 car (Car tour 9); park by the Refugio de Pineta (42° 39.968'N, 0° 6.212'E) for the standard walk, or — especially when there is a lot of water in the river — near the Camping Municipal (42° 40.554'N, 0° 5.171'E) for a longer itinerary which crosses the river by the bridge (as does the Alternative walk). Or take a taxi from Bielsa (10km/6mi; 619 71 79 93), asking to be dropped either on the road near the *refugio* or at the Camping Municipal. Return by 🚗 pre-arranged taxi or your car.
Useful contacts: Bielsa Tourist Office 974 50 11 27, bielsa.com; Parque Nacional Ordesa y Monte Perdido (at Pineta) 974 24 33 61; ordesamonteperdido.com; aragon.es
Short walk: Turn back any time you like — the views are spectacular all the way.
Alternative walk: Begin and end the walk at the *parador* (ⓑ), which will add almost 6km/3.7mi; 1h20min return.

Above: izard; below: Pineta Valley; below right: Tres Marías waterfall

Walk 24: Valle de Pineta and Punta del Valle 107

From the road beside the Río Cinca, you'd think that only an izard (Pyrenean chamois) could climb the almost-sheer cliffs of the Sierra de las Sucas on the opposite side of the valley. But it would be a pity to leave such stunning views to izards alone and, in fact, although steep, the path poses no great difficulty.

Finding the beginning of this walk caused readers plenty of problems over the years... before the advent of GPS. One foolproof method is to follow the Alternative walk and cross the Río Cinca by the BRIDGE just south of the PARADOR DE MONTE PERDIDO (**b**), beside the CAMPING MUNICIPAL (**a**). This automatically puts you on the **GR 11** in the **Valle de Pineta**, which this walk follows. If you are staying in either of these places, this makes sense but means hiking some 3km/2mi more than you have to *in each direction* (almost 6km/3.7mi in total).

We prefer, when the river is not running high, to **start the walk** at the **Refugio de Pineta** (**o**; by road, 2km before the Parador). In this case you need to rockhop or wade across the river, depending on the amount of water, aiming a little to the south of a WATERFALL on the far side. Once across, pick up the well-trodden **GR 11** (**1**) and follow it to the left.

Still wondering how to get up the sheer rock? In a few more minutes you will have the answer, as the cliff suddenly opens up to allow the path to enter the dense mixed forest, where it climbs steeply in a northwesterly direction.

Eventually you emerge in a CLEARING (**2**; **1h**) with a

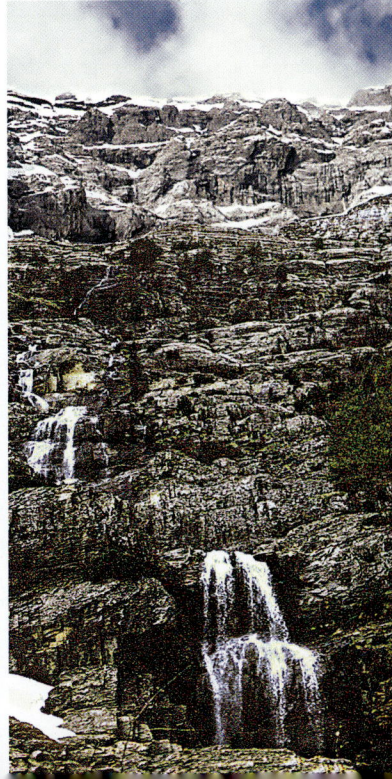

bewitching head-on view of the multi-tiered cliff faces of the **Tres Marías** waterfalls. If it's in full flow, the stream below these waterfalls is safe to drink (you'll need all the water you can get). Cross the stream on rocks and follow the path as it dives back into predominantly beech forest and becomes even steeper, requiring you to use your hands in several places.

After some **2h45min** the path emerges in a SECOND CLEARING, where there are some weirdly smooth cliffs above. (There's another opportunity to fill water bottles here.) Follow the path over the rocky shelves under the cliffs and up into an attractive MEADOW (❸), where you might see izards. Beyond the pasture the path zigzags up the line of a slight ridge. The *parador* is now clearly visible below, and some strange isolated cliffs, looking like ruins, rise to your right. Sit for a while and enjoy the spectacle.

Then climb towards the pass, with ever more vertiginous views. If you have the energy to go all the way to the **Collado de Añisclo** (❹) and on to the **Punta del Valle** (❺;

4h30min), your reward will be some glorious views of the Añisclo Canyon (Walk 25).

Descents sometimes take only half the time of ascents, but not in this case. Allow another *three hours* (**7h30min**) for the return, and don't be tempted to try any short cuts in the direction of the parador. The steep cliffs below you mean there are no short cuts!

La Ripareta (Walk 25)

Walk 25: THE AÑISCLO CANYON

See photo opposite
Distance: 16km/10mi; 5h30min
Grade: ●! easy climb of some 400m/1310ft, but sure-footedness and a head for heights essential
Equipment: no special equipment necessary — but see introductory notes on 'Walking', page 38.
Transport: 🚗 Park at the entrance to the canyon (San Úrbez car park; 42° 33.535'N, 0° 3.006'E), some 12.5km/8mi west of Escalona, along the road (HU631) to Sarvisé (see Car tour 9). This very narrow road is one-way (east to west): if you are approaching from Sarvisé, you will have to make a 30 minute detour via Buerba and Puyarruego (compensated by wonderful views over the canyon). The road is not suitable for nervous drivers or passengers.
Useful contacts: Huesca Tourist Office 974 29 21 70 (huesca turismo.com); Parque Nacional de Ordesa y Monte Perdido (at Escalona) 974 50 51 31, aragon.es
Short walk: ● Walk as far as you like along the canyon and return by the same route; the first hour is easy and not vertiginous.

The massifs of Monte Perdido (the highest limestone mountain in Europe) and the Sierra de Guara to the south are riddled with canyons, of which the Ordesa (see Walk 26) is the largest and most famous. Some of the other gorges are accessible only to those who descend the falls using wet suits and ropes (giving rise to the sport of 'canyoning'). The Añisclo Canyon lies somewhere in between these extremes — it's intimate, but easy.

Start out from the parking place near the ENTRANCE TO THE **Añisclo Canyon** (**O**). Follow the green signpost with a yellow arrow, taking a path towards *'PUENTE Y ERMITA DE SAN ÚRBEZ'*. When you meet a track by a signpost, follow it to the left. Cross the gorge by the concrete BRIDGE (**1**) and continue on the track, which has a precipitous drop to the left. You pass a CAVE 'CHAPEL' (**Ermita de San Úrbez**; **2**; **10min**) to your right, above the confluence of the **Río Aso** and the **Río Vellos** (**Bellos**). The track descends into the canyon to cross the Vellos by a concrete BRIDGE (**3**; **30min**). The route now narrows to a path that keeps the river on the right and begins to climb quite steeply.

Keep right at a signposted fork and then cross a side-stream on a metal BRIDGE (**4**; **40min**). Another seven minutes brings you above an exciting-looking water chute — the sort 'canyoners' whoosh down. After **1h** pass under an overhanging cliff. A further ten minutes brings you to a SPRING (**5**), where the water is safe to drink. The vegetation in the canyon is predominantly box, beech and oak — of which there are several types, including a Pyrenean variety which has white down on the undersides of the leaves.

After about **1h15min** reach a slightly 'delicate' part of the walk — a narrow, smooth and slippery section of rock with a steep fall to the right into the canyon below. On our first visit it was unguarded; on our last visit some none-too-solid looking posts and a wire had been erected. If you relax, there's no real difficulty. *Carefully* make your way to the far side. Climb past giant yew trees and reach a second (easier) gully crossing. The path gently undulates, keeping the precipitous drop to the right. The river flows below you — always within earshot. After **1h35min** you'll glimpse a magnificent WATERFALL (**6**) gushing through a narrow defile and, at the same time, another freshwater SPRING beside the path. A couple of minutes later come to a section of path which has been improved with logs and 'cobble'-stones. The path is very steep for the next 25 minutes, until it levels out in a small wood (**2h**).

Now you feel very high up, as you look down to the bottom of the gorge and the river far below. Grey and orange cliffs still tower above

Griffon vulture (above) and lammergeier (left)

you, however. The path takes you round to the left, directly beneath these overhanging cliffs (here again the path has been secured with 'cobble'-stones). For the first time since entering the canyon, the path is not following the direct line of the river, but climbing in long zigzags up the wall of the gorge. You come to a CONCRETE AND METAL BRIDGE (**7**; **2h05min**) — the remains of its much prettier wooden forerunner can be seen below.

Another steep climbing section zigzags for 35 minutes (**2h40min**), rising through conifers, fern and bracken, until the path emerges on a wide GRASSY PLATEAU with a steep unprotected drop to the right. After **2h55min** come to a rocky section over a stream (often dry), past giant beech trees and moss-covered rocks. This is followed by another 'roller-coaster' of ups and downs. The river comes into view again, and the way gradually descends towards the water's edge. Ahead are the spectacular mountains ringing the Ordesa Canyon.

Soon you come to **La Ripareta** (**8**; **3h10min**), the wide grassy plain shown on page 108, level with the river and surrounded by the canyon walls. While we choose to end the walk here, it is possible to follow the path to the end of the canyon, to the Fon Blanca waterfall (add 2h *each way*).

To return, retrace steps to the SIGNPOST (**5h30min**).

Walk 26: ORDESA — THE GRAND CANYON WALK

See also photos on pages 2, 30-31 and the cover
Distance: 19km/11.8mi; 5h30min
Grade: ●! easy outward leg (ascent of 450m/1475ft). The return is more demanding (ascent of 250m/820ft and steep, stony descent of 700m/2300ft); those unnerved by heights should return by the outward route and not by the Faja de Pelay which, in any case, should never be attempted when there is snow (September to June).

Some GR waymarking
Equipment: stout shoes; but see also notes on 'Walking', page 38.
Transport: 🚐 From Easter until mid-October there is a bus service from Torla-Ordesa to the Pradera de Ordesa (the starting point for the walk), from 06.00 until 21.00, with a peak time frequency of 15 minutes. Or 🚗 (Car tour 9). At Easter, from end-June to mid-Sep, and around 10 Oct, motorists are obliged to park at Torla and take the

Cascada de Cola de Caballo

bus (see above). The rest of the year, motorists can use the Pradera de Ordesa car park, the starting point for the walk (42° 38.969'N, 0° 3.608'E). *Note that when the park is deemed full (1800 visitors) the bus service is suspended.* For any further information call the Parque Nacional de Ordesa y Monte Perdido at Torla-Ordesa (974 24 33 61, aragon.es).
Short walk: Follow the footpath as far as the bridge (❸; **Puente de Arripas**) above the **Cascada del Abanico**, then return along the opposite bank of the Arazas River (2h; ● easy, almost level walk).
Alternative walk: Extend the walk by climbing the ● **Circo de Soaso** to the **Refugio Góriz** (ⓓ; add 450m/1475ft of ascent; 2h30min return), where it is possible to stay the night (telephone 974 34 12 01, goriz.es). See notes on page 114.

If you had to choose just one walk in the Pyrenees, this should be it. Amidst unforgettable canyon scenery, the track leads you to the foot of Monte Perdido, the third highest mountain in the range. The rocks themselves are a main attraction — endless calcareous cliffs, traversed by awesome stone balconies (known as *fajas*). But there is also the chance to see rare birds such as lammergeiers, griffon vultures and wallcreepers — while it is almost certain that you will spot izards (Pyrenean chamois).

From the **Pradera de Ordesa** CAR PARK (○): take the **GR 11** track east (signposted 'CASCADAS COLA CABALLO'). It runs at a short distance from the **Río Arazas**, and the sheer canyon walls rise 1000 metres (almost 3500 feet) above you on both sides. At a crossing of paths, follow signs for 'SOASO/REFUGIO GÓRIZ'. After **10min** you'll glimpse on your left the ROUTE TO THE CIRCO DE COTATUERO (❶) — worth trying if you're in the area for several days, *but not if you suffer from vertigo!*

The track, flat at first, continues under the dense canopy of a marvellous beech forest. The way then rises gently towards the **Cascada del Abanico** (❷; **40min**), beyond which those doing the Short walk may cross the river on the **Puente de Arripas** (❸). From here the track climbs more

Río Arazas

steeply, eventually emerging from the dense part of the forest to spectacular views of the canyon walls above and a series of waterfalls below.

After **1h30min** the walk levels out, and you keep the attractive Río Arazas on your right. Soon the valley widens, and the huge bulk of Monte Perdido is ahead. Eventually you come to the **Refugio de los Pastores** (❹; **2h15min**), from which the *circo* is now clearly visible. As you approach the **Circo de Soaso** (a rock amphitheatre associated with glaciation), the famous **Cascada de Cola de Caballo** comes into view to the left, looking — just as its name implies — exactly like a horse's tail (❺; **2h30min**).

The main walk now returns along the **Faja de Pelay**, one of the famous rock shelves for which the canyon is renowned. You cross the **Puente de Soaso** (❻) and your clearly marked path climbs slowly from the *circo*, past both paths to the Refugio Góriz *(see the Alternative walk overleaf)*. You rise up the **Senda de los Cazadores**, on the opposite side of the valley to your outward route. After 10 minutes a SIGN (❼; **2h40min**) warns you not to start out after 15.00h — you don't want to be negotiating this narrow path after dark. After 18 minutes (**2h48min**) the path levels out.

You pass above a tiered waterfall, the **Gradas de Soaso** (**3h**), with its clear green pools and foamy cascades, after which the path begins to climb more steeply. Watch out for loose stones. By **3h10min** you catch your first giddying glimpse of the car park, far, far below. The spectacular path continues through woods of birch, beech and pine until you arrive at a REFUGE AND VIEWPOINT (**8**; **4h36min**). You are now directly above the car park. The obvious descent past cliffs and through woods starts here. Be warned: the way is steep and stony, in several places badly eroded. You arrive back at the **Pradera de Ordesa** in **5h30min**.

Alternative walk — ascent to the Refugio Góriz

From the **Puente de Soaso** there are two ways up and onwards to the Refugio Góriz. You can choose between the SCREE PATH (**b**) that zigzags up the side of the *circo* in a southeasterly direction, and the direct assault — via the *'clavijas'* (**a**). The former looks impossible, but is merely arduous; the latter looks miraculous, but is merely terrifying!

If you choose the scree, you will find that although the path is invisible from a distance, it is clear close-up, and marked at intervals with the red and white paint stripes of the **GR 11**. The route via the *clavijas* involves a section assisted by a chain fixed to the rock by pegs and wire, and with a little of what climbers call 'exposure'. In reality, it isn't difficult, but anyone nervous of heights or carrying a heavy pack should stick to the scree path.

The two routes join up towards the top of the *circo* and, by either way, you will find yourself on a BROAD SHELF with the radio mast of the Refugio Góriz just visible almost due north (**c**; **1h**). This is an excellent spot for seeing izards, too: they are accustomed to walkers here and don't flee as quickly as those in the more remote areas of the range ... but don't waste their energy by trying to get too close to them.

Continue ascending the terraces in the general direction of the aerial, watching for red and white paint stripes (and sometimes flags, when there is snow on the ground).

The **Refugio de Góriz** (**d**) gradually reveals itself nestling at the foot of Monte Perdido, at a height of 2160m/7085ft. In **1h30min** you can be enjoying a drink or a meal — or perhaps a bunk in one of the dormitories. It is open all year; in winter the two guardians ski in with the provisions via the Cuello Gordo and the track to Nerín. In summer the hut can be bursting at the seams.

Walk 27: PIC D'ANIE

See also photo on page 32
Distance: 14km/8.7mi; 6h30min
Grade: 🔴 moderate, but with a strenuous 1060m/3477ft of ascent for the full itinerary; partly GR waymarked, partly cairns
Equipment: You will be climbing to 2504m/8213ft, so proper mountain walking equipment is essential (see introductory notes on 'Walking', page 38).
Transport: The starting point is easily reached only by 🚗 (Car tour 10). At Lescun follow signs to the *gîte d'étape* and continue on a narrow but good track to a small parking area just before the Refuge de Labérouat (42° 57.018'N, 0° 39.898'W). Or 🚌 to Lescun-Cette-Eygun (service Pau–Canfranc: sncf-connect.com; tel: 01 84919191), then taxi (09 88 29 03 38 fixed; 06 82 20 44 10 mobile) about 12km to the Refuge de Labérouat (05 59 34 71 67).
Other useful contacts: Vallée d'Aspe Tourist Office 05 59 34 57 57, tourisme-aspe.com
Shorter walks: Turn back at the **Cabane du Cap de la Baigt** (❷; 2h return; 🔵) or the **Col des Anies** (❹; 4h40min return; 🔴).
Alternative walk: From the **Cabane du Cap de la Baigt** (❷) instead of taking the left-hand path, you can turn *right* and follow the **GR 10** north to the **Pas d'Azuns** (ⓐ; 45min; 🔴), followed by a slightly more testing 30 minute climb and scramble for the reward of spectacular views from the **Pas d'Osque** (ⓑ; 1h 15min; ⚫).

Looking east from the Col des Anies

116   Landscapes of the Pyrenees

There is a magic about Lescun and its setting — at the end of a winding road, looking out over fields to coniferous forests and, to the west, the startling limestone scenery of the Pic d'Anie region. (Car tour 10 takes you around the other side of the Pic d'Anie, where the limestone formations are even more incredible.) It's not surprising that the forests round here were the last refuge of the indigenous brown bears and are now home to bears reintroduced from Slovenia.

Start out from the **Refuge de Labérouat** (⓿). Pass in front of the refuge and after **2min** pick up the clear red and white paint flashes of the **GR 10**, ignoring all other paths. The woods afford occasional glimpses of high mountains ahead and the bizarre cliffs of **Les Orgues**

Below: Les Orgues de Camplong, near the Refuge de Labérouat

de Camplong to the right. Just beyond the woods, you pass the **Cabane d'Ardinet** (❶; **55min**). By looking back down the valley you have just climbed you'll see the celebrated Pic du Midi d'Ossau in the far distance.

Continue following the well-marked path until you arrive at the **Cabane du Cap de la Baigt** (1689m/5540ft; ❷; **1h15min**), where we *leave* the GR10. You can retrace your steps from here to return to your car in a total of 2h *(Shorter walk)*. The main walk turns left (southwest) here, to follow the left bank of the stream (that is, keeping it on your left). After seven minutes (**1h22min**) cross the stream and continue zigzagging up for just under 40 minutes, to arrive at a flat pasture with a SMALL LAKE (**2h**). The Pic d'Anie looms to the left.

Continue along the path for two more minutes, at which point you will pass a large BROKEN LIMESTONE BLOCK. From here the path climbs steeply to the right, to join the scree slopes below the **Pic du Soum Couy**. Watch out for small cairn path markers and red and white flashes — you are now on the **HRP** (❸). After just over half an hour you will arrive at the **Col des Anies** (2084m/6836ft; ❹; **2h35min**), with an impressive view of Pic d'Arlas to the west. From here it's just 1.5km/0.9mi to the summit — but another 420m of ascent! *Leave* the HRP and head southwards

Walk 27: Pic d'Anie

towards the summit. The path has various paint marks and occasional cairns. It curls around the west side of the peak, to attack the summit from the south.

From the **Pic d'Anie** (⑤; 2504m/8213ft; **4h**) you will enjoy an immense panorama — as far as the sea on a clear day and to Vignemale in the opposite direction. Return to **Refuge de Labérouat** by the same route (**6h30min**).

Pic de Coutendé

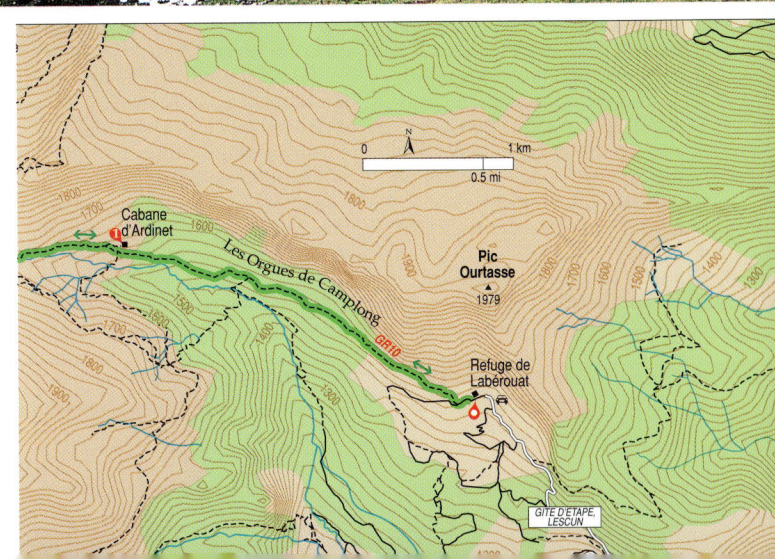

Walk 28: THE SONG OF ROLAND (MT ASTOBIZKAR)

The map continues overleaf
Distance: 16km/10mi; 5h35min
Grade: ● easy walking, with overall ascents of 420m/1380ft — but there are sections where the path is indistinct and where good orientation skills would be helpful: see 'Equipment' below. Some HRP/Camino de Santiago waymarking
Equipment: A compass/GPS is recommended for those sections over limestone rubble, known locally as *lapiaz,* where the path is invisible. If you stray from the path in this generally open terrain, you can usually cut across the open countryside to get back on course.
Transport: 🚗 From St-Jean-Pied-de-Port take the D301 to Estérencuby and, 3km/1.8mi further on, fork right on the D428. After a further 7km/4.3mi, watch for a track on the left which heads south to the nearby Col d'Orgambidé. Park on the grass just across the frontier (on the Spanish side of the col; 43° 2.965'N, 1° 12.689'W).
Useful contacts: St-Jean-Pied-de-Port Tourist Office 05 59 37 00 92, st-jean-pied-de-port.fr; Taxi 06 61 96 04 76, expressbourricot.com
Short walk: ● Return to your car from the **Col d'Arnostéguy** (❸), following the main walk from the 4h15min-point (8km/5mi; 3h).

This is a walking geography and history lesson. The geography includes bizarre limestone scenery, while the history embraces cromlechs and a route that has variously been followed by the Romans during the conquest of northern Spain, pilgrims to Santiago, and Napoleon's troops. But, most famously of all, Charlemagne's army was ambushed here after the sacking of Pamplona, an event celebrated in the medieval poem, the *Song of Roland*.

Start out at the **Col d'Orgambidé** (⭕): follow a white concrete track opposite the parking place. After 200m, leave the concrete track for a gravel track on the right that you follow northwestwards. This narrows to a footpath and alternates between forest and open grassland where *dolines* (funnel-shaped depressions) and limestone rubble set traps for the unwary. The path becomes fainter and fainter as it climbs steadily along a small valley on the southern side of the frontier. (Eventually the frontier will be crossed between marker stones 207 and 208.)

After **1h** a particularly large *doline* confirms that you are on course, forcing you leftwards, up a small hill. From the top you should be able to see the **Cabane d'Urculu**, a small house, to the north. Turn away from the *cabane* and head due south, climbing to a ridge and then on up to the SUMMIT of **Urculu** (1419m/4654ft; ❶; **1h30min**). If you are in the right place you will be just above the low ruins of a ROUND STONE TOWER (❷), which some experts date from Roman times and others as late as 1500AD.

Descend southwest along the line of the frontier to the **Col d'Arnostéguy** (❸; **1h40min**), where the D428 comes up from St-Jean-Pied-de-Port. *(Those following the Short walk can return from here by picking up the notes from the 4h15min-point below.)*

To continue the main walk, follow the **HRP** (red and white stripes) westwards along the French side of the frontier. After 30 minutes the path crosses to the Spanish side close to the **Col de Bentarte** (❹;

2h10min). This is one possible site for the ambush of Charlemagne's rearguard. Continue southwest along the route of the old Roman road (see map overleaf), past the ruined chapel of **Elizaxare** (**5**; **2h25min**).

Where the trail cuts between two hills, break away to the right, pathless, to reach the SUMMIT of **Astobizkar** (1506m/4940ft; **6**; **3h**). Looking southwest from the top you will see the Puerto de Ibañeta, the most likely scene of the battle, where, in the *Song*, the dying Roland tried to break his sword Durandel (and in so doing created the Brèche de Roland!; Walk 22).

Now retrace your steps as far as the **Col d'Arnostéguy** (**3**; **4h 15min**). Here we follow the **HRP/ GR 12** red and white waymarkings along a dirt track heading eastwards into another col, the **Collado Soroluze** (**7**; **4h30min**). About fifty paces off to the right is a RUINED DOLMEN and, a little further on, a CROMLECH of 16 stones (**8**), dating from about 2000BC.

After a further 20 minutes the HRP brings you to some CABINS (**4h50min**). Just beyond them, at a DRINKING TROUGH, take the grassy path to the left (northeastwards) just before the road (still the HRP). (There may be a sign here,

Memorial to Roland at the Puerto de Ibañeta

'COLLADO DE AZPEGI'.) Eventually you pass a SPRING with a sign, 'FUENTE ARRATAKAS, 970M' (**5h20min**). Some 200m off to the left lies a second CROMLECH (**9**), this time of 11 stones. Continue along the track and regain your car near the **Col d'Orgambidé** after **5h35min**.

Walk 29: RONCESVALLES

See photo on page 118
Distance: 18.5km/11.5mi; 5h50min
Grade: 🔴 easy walking, with overall ascents of 500m/1640ft, but there are sections where the path is indistinct and where good orientation skills would be helpful: see 'Equipment' below. Some HRP/Camino de Santiago waymarking
Equipment: A compass/GPS is mended for those sections over limestone rubble; see comments for Walk 28 on page 118.
Transport: 🚐 from Pamplona to Roncesvalles (Autocars Artieda: 948 30 02 87, autocaresartieda.com — tickets only available on the day at the bus station). At Roncesvalles you can follow the path taken by pilgrims returning from Santiago de Compostela, heading northeast up to the Collado Lepoeder. It is waymarked with scallop shells and yellow arrows. Add 500m/1640ft; 3h return to the times given for motorists. Or 🚖 taxi (from France 06 61 96 04 76, expressbourricot.com, or from Spain 948 23 23 00, taxipamplona.com) to the Collado Lepoeder, following the directions for motorists below. For information about public transport and taxis telephone the Pamplona Tourist Office: 948 420 700, turismo.navarra.es. Or 🚗 (Car tour 11). After visiting Roncesvalles, continue northwards and just before the frontier, at the Puerto de Ibañeta, turn right along the tarmac road which leads to the radio mast on Monte Ortzanzurieta. After 2.5km/1.6mi park at the Collado Lepoeder (where a track goes off to the left; 43° 1.576'N, 1° 17.722'W).

Shorter walks

1 🔴; 4h return. Follow the main walk to the **Col d'Arnostéguy** (**3**) and the CROMLECH (**8**) 15 minutes past it. Then retrace your steps, but deviate to the stone tower (**2**) on **Urculu**.

2 11km/6.8mi; 4h; 🔵 easy, with an ascent of 550m/1800ft. From **Roncesvalles** (**b**), follow notes for those who come by bus to reach the **Collado Lepoeder** (**O**). Walk to **Astobizkar** (**6**), then return and follow the **HRP** west to (**a**), the

Walk 29: Roncesvalles 121

Puerto de Ibañeta, where you will see the memorial to Roland shown on page 118). From here a waymarked path descends to **Roncesvalles** (**b**). Useful information: Roncesvalles Museum:

Burguete was once the haunt of Ernest Hemingway, whose early novel, *Fiesta*, describes how he first saw 'the red roofs and white houses of Burguete ... and away off on the shoulder of the first dark mountain ... the grey metal-sheathed roof of the monastery of Roncesvalles'. Roncesvalles (Roncevaux to the French) claims relics of the battle, 'celebrated' in the medieval *Song of Roland*, that wiped out Charlemagne's rearguard. You can learn more before setting off on your walk by taking the guided tour of Roncesvalles' museum and treasures.

Our timings start at the **Collado Lepoeder** (**O**): Ignore the track heading north (it is the **HRP** and also the **Camino de Santiago**; you will join it soon). Instead, for the moment, climb the grassy trail at the left of the track. When the trail peters out, keep ahead (due north) to the SUMMIT of **Astobizkar** (1506m/4940ft; **6**; **10min**), where you join Walk 28. This is a brief resume with the main timings for those starting from the Collado Lepoeder. For a full description, refer to Walk 28.

From Astobizkar drop back down eastwards, pathless, to rejoin the track. The Camino de Santiago veers off north at the **Col de Bentarte**, but you are still on the **HRP**: follow its red and white waymarks to the **Col d'Arnostéguy** (**3**; **1h25min**), where the D428 comes up from St-Jean-Pied-de-Port.

Now follow Walk 28 from the 4h15min-point (page 119) at **3** to the **Col d'Orgambidé** (**O**; **2h45min**), starting point for Walk 28. Then pick up the notes for the beginning of Walk 28, to bring you back to **Col d'Arnostéguy** once more (**3**; **4h25min**) and, from there, retrace your steps to the **Collado Lepoeder** (**5h50min**).

Walk 30: IPARLA RIDGE

Distance: 10.4km/6.5mi; 6h30min
Grade: 🔴❗ very strenuous if you go all the way to the top — 900m/2952ft of ascent; GR waymarking
Equipment: the area is prone to mist; see 'Walking', page 38.
Transport: 🚍+🚌 to Bidarray Pont Noblia (SNCF line 62, changing to an SNCF bus at Cambo-les-Bains): freephone within France 0800 872 872, sncf-connect.com), then cross the river by the bridge, turn left, and walk up to the town hall ('Herriko Etxea'). Or 🚗: Car tour 12; park at the town hall ('Herriko Etxea') in Bidarray Pont Noblia (43° 15.935'N, 1° 20.964'W). For a taxi telephone 06 78 34 49 90 or 06 78 34 49 90. For general information call the Hendaye Tourist Office 05 59 20 00 34,

Walk 30: Iparla Ridge 123

hendaye-tourisme.fr. Return on line 62 🚐 from Bidarray, then 🚌 from Cambo, or 🚕.
Short walk: Hike just far enough to enjoy the views and return the same way (🔵; about 3h return).
Alternative walk: Continue along the ridge from Pic d'Iparla as far as the **Col d'Harrieta** (🅰; 808m/2650ft), then quit the GR 10 to take a waymarked path down to **Urdos** (🅱). Allow about 2h30min to descend from the peak to Urdos (total 12km/7.4mi; 6h30min), from where you will have to take a taxi back to your car, or to a railway station (the nearest is St-Martin d'Arrossa, about 8km). 🔴❗ Grade as main walk.

The Iparla Ridge (Crête d'Iparla) is a classic walk in the Basque country, the domain of black and griffon vultures. It is also part of the GR10 long-distance footpath, marked by red and white flashes.

Start out from the TOWN HALL (⭕; 'Herriko Etxea') at **Bidarray**. Walk up the hill, and either follow the signpost 'IPARLA', forking *right* almost at once (the new route of the **GR 10**) or follow us: fork *left* here, keeping the Gîte Mediterrena to your right). Both routes are shown

Iparla Ridge from near Bidarray

on the map and both are on the GPS track file.

If taking the new GR 10, just follow the signs and the red and white flashes. If following our old route, the road will divide again after a few minutes. Go right, climbing gently, until at **7min** you pass — and ignore — another turn to the right.

Soon after follow a faded red footpath arrow round to the right, until you come to **Urdabordia**, a large farmhouse, where the tarmac ends (❶; **15min**). Now join a wide earthen track which sweeps around to the left, through the farmyard and then becomes a steeply-climbing path.

Our route and the new **GR 10** join forces shortly past the farmhouse and move on past a RUIN (❷; **55min** — or a bit longer with the newer route). The way is now clearly marked with red and white flashes, climbing up the ridge with its all-round views, through woods, across a grassy bowl, and up to a HIGH POINT (**1h45min**).

From now on you have another choice: you can stick to the path along the cliff edge (**Crête d'Iparla**), for the frisson that comes with 'exposure', or you can bear away a little into the grass. Ignore the vultures wheeling overhead — it's nothing personal.

If you've ever wondered what it's like to soar high above the ground on a *parapente*, the path to the summit will give you a fair idea. You can't go wrong — just follow the cliff. At the SUMMIT of **Pic d'Iparla** (1044m/3424ft; ❸; **4h**) your efforts are rewarded; the views are exhilarating — and terrifying.

Return the same way, or continue along the ridge for the Alternative walk. Whichever route you choose, you will be back down in either **Bidarray** or **Urdos** (ⓑ) in about 2h30min (total **6h30min**).

Walk 31: CIRCUIT BASED ON BIRIATOU

Distance: 14.5km/9mi; 4h30min
Grade: ● moderate climb/ descent of 450m/1475ft; GR/ HRP and local waymarking
Equipment: water; see also introductory notes on 'Walking', page 38.
Transport: 🚆 to Hendaye (Toulouse to St-Jean-de-Luz line): freephone within France 0800 872 872, sncf-connect.com, then taxi: 05 59 20 20 30 or 06 81 00 52 16 to Biriatou. Or 🚗: Car tour 12; park at Biriatou car parking area (43° 20.016'N, 1° 44.573'W). For general information telephone the Hendaye Tourist Office 05 59 20 00 34, hendaye-tourisme.fr. Return by 🚗 taxi from Biriatou back to Hendaye station, or 🚆
Alternative walks: Three itineraries are described for this area. By referring to the paths and tracks on the map on pages 126-127, as well as Walks 32 and 33, you can make up your own alternatives.

Biriatou is a hilltop village notable for its splendid church (designated *'site classé'* in French conservation terms) and the unusual location of its *fronton* (pelota court) — it's joined onto the village *auberge*.

Start the walk at the CAR PARK in **Biriatou** (⭕), climbing the hill to the CHURCH and the *fronton* beside AUBERGE HIRIBARREN (both players and ball move like lightning so, if a game is in progress, watch out!). Take the alley beside the *auberge* and turn left on a tarmac road. Notice — but ignore — any local path waymarking; keep to the (perhaps faded) red/white waymarks of the **GR 10**/**HRP**.

After **8min**, at a sharp bend, take the signposted lane to the right (the road ahead is marked with both orange and yellow ✗s. This lane divides almost immediately: take the ascending lane to the right, ignoring the cart track on the left. In **10min** the tarmac surface ends, just past a large house on the right. Continue ahead to a fork and go right on a trail with the same waymarks in a signpost (a parking area is signed off to the left). The trail bends right, then left, then curves round to the right past a concrete WATER-PUMPING STATION (❶; **12min**). Ahead you'll see the cliffs of the **Rocher des Perdrix** ('Partridge Rock'), a wild landscape marred only by the giant electricity pylons.

Some 200m past the pumping station the path divides. The GR 10 goes right; keep left with the **HRP**. The path turns sharp right, then immediately forks sharp left uphill, to pass just to the right of one of the PYLONS (❷; **20min**). After a few minutes (300 metres) the path sweeps around to the right (ignore the branch to the left), and the way now continues along the bottom of the cliffs. The path alternates between mud and stone, often with rocks and boulders 'cemented' into extraordinary pebble-dashed spheres, known as conglomerates.

Eventually you arrive at a wide grassy plateau, the **Col d'Osin** (❸; **1h**). Walk over the pass in a fairly straight line. A clear view of a lake (**Lac de Xoldokogaina**; sometimes dried up) opens up on your left.

The GR 10 rejoins from the right at the **Col des Poiriers** (❹; **1h10min**). Those wanting a short walk can now turn left off the main

Left: Walks 31 and 32: fields near Biriatou

path, head down to the lake, picnic and retrace their steps. Those continuing on the main walk should follow the path that keeps the small larch wood on the immediate right. Here the marked path moves close to the wood and climbs for 15 minutes until it reaches a definite U-shaped dip, the **Col des Joncs** (**5**; **1h 25min**). From here you enjoy new vistas southwards to the Bidasoa (Bidassoa in French) River. Some 15 minutes from the Col des Joncs the red- and white-marked **GR 10/ HRP** swings sharply left, but you follow a new path to the right, almost immediately CROSSING A SMALL STREAM (**6**; **1h 40min**).

Walk 31: Circuit based on Biriatou 127

Follow this path until, at **1h50min**, you reach an impressive RIDGE with splendid views all around. Your walk will head right here, but first take a ten-minute diversion to the left, to see the **Ancien Redoute** (fortified stronghold) **de la Bayonnette** (**7**; **2h**). Close by is FRONTIER STONE 9, a place where you can straddle the Franco-Spanish border (see photo on page 131). Return to the ridge-top crossroads where you started your diversion and follow the line of the ridge southwest as it descends towards the valley and the **Bidasoa River**.

Continue descending and ignore any vehicle tracks joining from the

The church at Biriatou, with the mairie to the left and the auberge to the right (above) and (right): La Rhune from the Col d'Osin (Walks 31 and 32)

Spanish side. You do not want any of these, however tempting they may look; stay instead on the WAYMARKED PATH, reaching an old RUIN at **2h25min**. After about five minutes of gentle descent, come to a PLANTATION OF OAKS (**8**; **2h30min**). Here the path starts to descend much more steeply, in places becoming quite difficult. You may noticed faded paint flashes on trees.

At the bottom of the path you may have to negotiate a FENCE — either by a stile or by climbing over. Then turn right along a vehicle track, almost immediately fording a stream. Continue to follow the track, with the stream on your right. The track is flat at first but then zigzags up to a farm called 'LIZARLAN' (**9**; **3h30min**). Continue from here to a tarmac road (**4h**) and follow it straight ahead.

At about **4h20min**, opposite a parking and picnic area on your left, you should spot a narrow path on the right that climbs up obliquely from the road, through trees, to regain the CHURCH and CAR PARK at **Biriatou** (**4h30min**). If you don't spot it, there is a better, signposted path 300m further on. If you take the latter path, turn right to the CAR PARK when you reach the road.

Walk 32: XOLDOKOGAINA (CHOLDOKOGAGNA)

See also photos opposite
Distance: 15km/9.5mi; 4h10min
Grade: ● easy climbs of about 600m/1970ft overall; GR/HRP and local waymarking
Equipment: no special equipment necessary — but see introductory notes on 'Walking', page 38.
Transport: 🚌 to Hendaye; then 🚗 taxi or car to Biriatou (see Walk 31).

However, it is possible to shorten this walk some 2.5km/1h by starting at the Col d'Ibardin: follow *Walk 33*, but turn *right* when you join the lakeside track beyond the short-cut path (❶ in Walk 33). Return by the same transport from Biriatou or the Col d'Ibardin
Alternative walks: See Walk 31.

The highest peak in the Basque country, La Rhune, is unfortunately spoilt for walkers by its rack railway and radio mast. Try instead this delightful itinerary: it takes you through a varied landscape to a panoramic viewpoint.

Start out by following **Walk 31** as far as the **Col des Poiriers** (❹; **1h10min**). At the pass, take the track off left down to the **Lac de Xoldokogaina** and follow it along the southern shore, through tree plantations. It climbs to join a well-made track coming from the right (**1h45min**). Turn left and follow this new track for eight minutes (**1h53min**), until a further track comes up, heading obliquely back left, towards the dam. Follow this track to the **DAM** (❺; **1h58min**), cross it, and then take a track heading right (north). It runs along the side of a valley, above the **Arolako Erreka River**. The way at first falls, but then climbs to the TOP OF A RIDGE, reached some 30 minutes from the dam (**2h30min**). Cross over the ridge and drop down to the tarmac road on the other side. Follow the tarmac/then path in a hairpin bend away from the gated-off WATER FILTRATION PLANT (❻), to a grassy PARKING AREA (❼; **2h35min**).

From here several trails lead off, and to add to the confusion, when last checked there were *no* signs or waymarks. The path you want leaves the parking area in a south-southwesterly direction. It climbs

View to the Lac de Xoldokogaina through mist

towards the summit of a mountain (Xoldokogaina), *but keeps the ridge a little to the left*. (There is a path along the ridge as well.) You may see faded BLUE PAINT MARKS on this path.

Some 45 minutes from the parking area, you reach the rounded summit of **Xoldokogaina** (Choldokogagna; 486m/1595ft; ❽; **3h20min**), with its 'slingshot' trig point marker stone. After enjoying the views to the sea and inland to La Rhune and beyond, descend southeast on the clear path that leads back to the **Col d'Osin** (❸; **3h30min**). Having regained your outgoing route, turn right to retrace your steps to **Biriatou (4h10min)**.

Left: an important crossroads for Walks 31, 32, 33: the Col des Poiriers

Walk 33: COL D'IBARDIN

See map opposite; see also photos on page 129 and 130
Distance: 8km/5mi; 2h15min
Grade: ● easy climb of about 300m/1000ft; local waymarking
Equipment: nothing necessary
Transport: The Col d'Ibardin is a mini-Andorra on the Franco-Spanish frontier, a place the French love to visit for weekend shopping expeditions. Reach it by taxi (in Spain 943 63 33 03, radiotaxibidasoa.com, or, in France 05 59 54 63 93). By car take the road up from Spain via Vera de Bidasoa or, from France, the D4/D404 from the coast (via Urrugne). Or detour from Ascain on Car tour 12; park just before the shops (43° 18.574'N, 1° 41.210'W).
For general information contact the Urrugne Tourist Office 05 59 54 60 80, en-pays-basques.fr
Alternative walk: See Alternative walk 31, page 125.

The Col d'Ibardin is on the famous Haute Route Pyrénées, but we suggest an easy itinerary that everyone can enjoy. It takes you through magnificent plantations and around the lake shown on page 129, Lake Xoldokogaina.

Start out from the CAR PARK just before the shops in the main shopping street (a cul-de-sac) at the **Col d'Ibardin**: take a signposted TRACK (**O**) off to the right. You'll pass a PICNIC PLACE (**❶**) within five minutes and then a signposted TRACK (**❷**) back to the right five minutes later.

Your level track winds among magnificent — if somewhat too regimented — plantations, and later beside a beautiful oak forest. In **25min** you have your first glimpse of a lake ahead and, a minute later, a painted arrow indicates a SHORT-CUT (**❸**) to the left. You'll join a LAKESIDE TRACK in a minute or two. Turn left on this track and follow it among the plantations, keeping the LAKE on your right. Beyond the lake you come to the **Col des Poiriers** (**❹**; **1h**), where you meet up with Walks 31 and 32.

To return to the Col d'Ibardin, turn left at the Col des Poiriers and skirt the larch forest, following Walk 31 (page 128) as far as the **Ancien Redoute de la Bayonnette** (**❼**; **1h50min**). From the *redoute* continue northeast, more or less along the ridge, until you regain the **Col d'Ibardin** (**2h15min**).

Walkers near frontier stone 9 and the Ancien Redoute de la Bayonnette, looking south towards the Peñas de Aia in Spain (Walks 31 and 33)

Walk 34: PEÑAS DE AIA (AIAKO HARRIA)

Distance: 9km/5.6mi; 3h (18km/11.2mi; 5h30min if you descend to Irún)

Grade: ●! This itinerary involves some rock-climbing, albeit of a fairly easy kind. For the full walk, you'll need your hands, agility and a head for heights. The highest peak is about 330m/1082ft above the parking area but, allowing for all the ups and downs, you'll do about 480m/1575ft of ascent. Local and GR waymarking

Equipment: suitable gripping footwear is essential; stout trainers are fine, but shoes with smooth soles must *not* be worn.

Transport: 🚆 to Irún (RENFE 91 2 320 320, renfe.com); then taxi (943 63 33 03, radiotaxibidasoa.com) from Irún station. Ask the taxi driver for the Peñas de Aia (Aiako Harria), then watch out for the parking spot suggested below for motorists. Or 🚗 (Car tour 12). Approaching Irún on the D810 from France, cross the Bidasoa River and at the roundabout take the GI636 which keeps the river on your right. At the next roundabout turn left following brown signs for Aiako Harria and then turn left again at the following roundabout (same signposting). After 150m/yds turn right (same signposting) and keep going for about 9km/5.5mi. Just after power lines cross, there is a large parking area on the left (43° 17.711'N, 1° 47.198'W). Return on foot to Irún station by one of the footpaths described on page 134 if you have not come by car.

Useful contacts: Irún Tourist Office 943 50 51 52, irun.org/turismo; basque country-tourism.com; bidasoaturismo.com; summer information point at Lapurrituri

Short walk: Those without a taste for rock-climbing can follow the itinerary as long as they feel comfortable, returning the same way.

Alternative walk: Paths skirting the peaks to the east and west are detailed on a signboard.

Walk 34: Peñas de Aia (Aiako Harria) 133

The Peñas de Aia are a landmark on the Spanish side of the border and a great spectacle, known in Basque as Aiako Harria and to the French as the 'Trois Couronnes' — the three crowns. They are protected with the status of 'parque natural' and are very popular with climbers, offering routes of various degrees of difficulty. Our itinerary follows paths suitable for fit, agile walkers and does not require special equipment or skills, other than a head for heights. We are going to walk and scramble right along the spine of the three peaks, returning by a path just below the summits to the west. If you have a fear of heights, just do the first part, or follow one of the lower itineraries shown on the board.

Start out from the PARKING AREA WITH SIGNBOARD below the **Peñas de Aia** (◯): follow the obvious path that heads southeastwards towards the peaks, passing just to the left of a PYLON. After **12min** come to a PILLBOX (❶) and follow the well-trodden path that zigzags beyond it, to arrive on a minor summit, **Muganix** (786m/2580ft; ❷; **30min**).

But you are not yet on one of the three peaks of Haya! For that privilege, drop down and continue along the ridge. The path passes an area where the rock is sharply tilted and the soil below to the left eroded into CAVES, while to the right there is an impressive drop. At **40min** the path divides; take the upper way, across an easy slab of rock, and come to the next summit, where a shrine announces '**Monte Irumugarrieta**, 806 METRES' (2645ft; ❸; **45min**). Congratulations! You have bagged your first Haya summit.

To continue along the ridge, drop back down over the rock slab to where the path divided and now take the lower path onward and up **Monte Txurrumurru** (826m/2710ft; ❹; **1h**).

From here on things get more tricky because there is a steep descent into a gully — and descents are always more unnerving that ascents. If it's not for you, turn back. Otherwise, climb down into the gully and up the opposite side, following the path along the ridge. At the far end the path zigzags down in a southeasterly direction to meet another path coming from the northeast, along a kind of 'toboggan run'. From here you climb southwestwards in a series of zigzags to the final summit, **Erroilbide** (836m/2745ft — also known as the path that descends in zigzags to the northeast until, at a height of around 700m, it swings almost due south above the trees and along a shelf, before once more descending to join the **GR 121 TRAIL** (**6**) coming from the Aritxulegi tunnel.

Turn right (northwards) along this path, which cuts through the trees and across the bottom of the gully known as the **Corredor de Bocamina**, to return to the PARKING AREA in 1h30min (**3h**).

Walking on down to Irún

If you came by taxi, there are three possible routes to take you the back to Irún. Only the new GR 11 route is way-marked, *but there are GPS tracks available for all three.*

You can take a track that begins on the opposite side of the road from the parking area, an old *sendero local* with some faded green/white waymarks in place (**a**). The track (9km) is loosely surfaced and in places descends steeply.

The other is the old GR 11 footpath, also 9km, where you may spot faded red/white stripes. To pick that up, walk along the road eastwards from the parking area for about 2.4km/1.4mi and then take a very narrow path descending left off the road (**b**).

(The *new* GR 11 footpath leaves the road to the *right* (**c**) 150m *before* the old path; the only walking sign, when last seen, was a pictogram of a dog on a lead. This path is beyond the edges of our map, and will cost you 11-12km.)

You should reach the STATION in **Irún** (**d**) in about **5h30min** or **6h**.

Monteaya; **5**; **1h30min**). The views over the sweep of Basque coastline from San Sebastián to Biarritz are superb.

You could return by retracing your steps, but we suggest taking

Index

Geographical names only are included here; for non-geographical entries, see Contents, page 3. A page number in *italic type* indicates a map reference; a page number in **bold type** a photograph or drawing; both may be in addition to a text reference on the same page. To save space, the following are indexed separately: mountains; cols; caves; rivers, valleys, gorges.

Agos Vidalos 27, 28
Aigües Tortes, Parc Nacional d' 23, **24**, 88-9, *89*
Ainhoa 35, 36
Amélie-les-Bains 14, 15
Ancien Redoute de la Bayonnette *126-7, 130,* **131**
Andorra la Vella 16-17
Ansó 31
Arette-Pierre-St Martin 31, 32, 33
Argelès-sur-Mer 12, *13*
Argelès-Gazost 27, 28
Arles-sur-Tech 15
Arreau 25, **26**
Arties 23
Ascain 36
Aspin-Aure 26
Aulus-les-Bains 21, 22
Ax-les-Thermes 18
Axiat 18
Bagnères-de-Bigorre 25, 26, 27, 28, 90
Bagnères-de-Luchon, see Luchon
Banyoles 14
Banyuls-sur-Mer 12, *13*, 51, *52-3,* **54**
Barèges 27, 28
Baronnies 25, **90, 91, 92**, *92*
Beaucens 27, 28, **37**
Bellver de Cerdanya 16
Besalú 14, **15**
Bidarray 35, 36, *122,* **123**, 124
Bielsa 29, 30, 106
Biriatou 36, **124-5,** *126-7,* **128,** 129, 130
Le Boulou 12, 13, 14, 15
Bourg-Madame 16
Broto 29
Buerba 29, 109
Bujaruelo 29
Burguete 33, 34, 121
Cadaqués 12, *48-9*
Cala Jóncols *48-9*, 50
Cala Montjoi *48-9*, 50
Caldes de Boí 23, **24**
Campan 26, 28
Camprodon 14, 15
Candanchú 31, 32
Canfranc 32
Cap de Norfeu *48-9*, **49**, 50

Castellfollit de la Roca 14, 58, 61
Castillon-en-Couserans 22
Cauterets 27, 28, 37, 103
Caves
  Bédeilhac 21, 22
  Bellevue **98**, 99
  Gargas 25
  Médous 26, 28
  Niaux 21
  Pierre-St Martin 32, 33
  Russell's Caves **98**, 99
Cerbère 12, *13*
Céret 14, 15
Col, pass, *port*
  Anies **115,** *116-7*
  Añisclo 106, *108*
  Arnostéguy *119, 120-121*
  Aspin 25, 26
  Belagua 31, 32
  Bonaigua 23
  Boucharo, see Gavarnie
  Brèche de Roland 28, 35, 36, *95,* **100-1,** *101,* 102
  Burdincurutcheta 33
  Envalira 16
  Ibañeta 33, 34, **118,** *120-1*
  Ibardin 36, *126-7,* 129, *130,* **131**
  Ispéguy 36
  Lepoeder *120-1*
  Marmare 18
  Monastero 88, *89*
  Orgambidé 118, *119, 120-1*
  Orgambidesca 33
  Osin **125,** *126-7,* **128,** *130*
  Ours **18-9**
  Peyresourde 25, 26
  Poiriers *126-7,* 128, 129, **130,** *130,* 131
  Port 22
  Tentes 100, *101,* 102
  Tourmalet 27, 28
  Trappe 22
  Venasque **92-3,** *93,* 94
Colera 13
Collioure 12, **13,** 51, *52-3*
Comus 18, 19, *80,* **81**
Cornellana 17
Dantxarinea 35, 36
Elizondo 35
Engolasters 74, *74-5*

Escaladieu, Abbaye d' 25, **91**
Les Escaldes *74-5,* 76
Escalona 29, 30
Escároz 34
Esparros 25, **90,** *92*
Espèche 25
Espelette 36
L'Espine 18, 20
Espolla 12
Espot 23, **24**
Esterri d'Aneu 23
Eus **10-1**
Eyharce 36
Fageda d'en Jordà 55, **56,** 57
Fanlo 29
Foix 18, **20**
Garriguella 12
Gavarnie 2, **26-7**, 28, *95,* 96, 97, 100, *101*
Gèdre 28
Gerri de la Sal 23
Girona 14
Goizueta 35
Gósol 16, 17, *71,* **72-3**
Gourbit *5*
Gréixer 17
Guardiola 16, 17
Guzet-Neige 22
Hecho 31
Hendaye 125, 129
Hernani 35
Hospice de France **93,** *94*
Hospital de Tella 29, 30
Irún *126-7,* 132, 133, *134*
Isaba 33
Itxassou 36
Jaca 31, 32
La Jonquera 12
Josa del Cadí **17**
Lakes, reservoirs, etc
  Artax (Artats) *85,* **85**
  Banyoles 14
  Comte 77, *78-9*
  Couart 77, *78-9*
  Engolasters *74-5,* **75**
  Gardelle 82, *83*
  Gaube 103, *104-5*
  Laparan 86, *87*
  Lers 21
  Monestero 88, *89*
  Nère *104-5*
  Ossoue **98,** 99

135

Pourtet 103, *104-5*
Sant Maurici 23, *89*
Soulcem 21, **82-3**, *83*
Vidal 77, *78-9*
Xoldokogaina (Cholokogagna) *126-7*, **129**, *130*
Laroque des Albères 13
Larrau 33
Laugibar 33
Lées-Athas 32
Lescun 31, **32**
Llançà 12, 45, *46-7*
Llavorsí 23
Llívia 16
Lomne 25
Lourdes 27, 28
Luchon (Bagnères de) 25, 26
Luz-St Sauveur 27, 28
Maçaners **8-9**, 17
Massat 21, 22
Mauvezin, Château de 25
Mérens-les-Vals 18, 77, *78-9*
La Mongie 27, 28
Montagut 14, 58, 61
Montaillou 18, 19
Montségur 18, **20**
Mountains, ridges, volcanoes, plateaus, rock formations, etc
 Albères 12-13
 Anie 33, 115, *116-7*
 Astobizkar 118, *119*, *120-1*
 Belh 86, *87*
 Cadí, Serra del **8-9**, 16, **17**, 71, **72-3**; Túnel del 23, 24
 Canigou **15**, *63*, **64**
 Coutendé **117**, *116-7*
 Croscat *55*, **56-7**
 Els Encantats **88-9**, *88-9*
 l'Estela, Serra de 45, *46-7*
 Garrotxa, La 14, *60*, 61, 62
 Gavarnie (Cirque de) 27, 28, *95*, **96-7**, *101*
 Iparla 36, *122*, **123**, 124
 Isards, Crête des 86, *87*, **87**
 Midi de Bigorre 28
 Orgues de Camplong **116**, *116-7*
 Pedraforca **8-9**, **17**, *71*, **72-3**
 Peguera 88, *89*
 Peñas de Aia (Aiako Harria) 36, *126-7*, **131**, **132-3**, *134*
 Perdido **30-1**, 112, *113*
 Pibeste 28
 Pineta (Circo de) 30
 Prade 27, *95*, *101*
 Rhune, La 35, 36, **128**
 Santa Margarida *55*, **56**, 57
 Sault **4**, 18, 20, *80*, **81**
 Sauvegarde 93, *94*
 Soaso (Circo de) **2**, **111**, *112-3*, 114

Taillon 100, *101*
Urculu 118, *119*, *120-1*
Vignemale *98*
Xoldokogaina (Cholokogagna) *126-7*, 129, 130
Niaux 21
Núria *68-9*, **70**
Ochagavía 33, 34
Olot 14, 55, 57
Ordesa, Parque Nacional de Ordesa y Monte Perdido **2**, 29, **111**, *112-3*, **113**
Oza, Selva de 31, **cover**
Pamplona 33, 34
Pierrefitte-Nestalas 28
La Pobla de Segur 23
La Pobleta de Bellvei 23, 24
Pont d'Espagne 103, *104-5*
Pont de Suert 23, 24
Portbou 12, 13
Port de la Selva 12
Port-Vendres 12, 13, *52-3*
Prades 19
Prats-de-Molló 14, 15
Puigcerda 16, 17
Puyarruego 29, 30
Pyrénées, Parc National des 32, 43, *95*, 96, *101*
Queralbs *68-9*, 70
Revilla 29, 30
Ribes de Freser 15, 17, 68
Ripoll **14**, 15
Rivers, streams, valleys, gorges, glaciers
 Añisclo 30, **108**, 109, *110*
 Ara 29
 Arazas *112-3*, **111**, **113**
 Ariège 21, 77, *78-9*
 Aso 29, 109, *110*
 Aspe 31
 Aston *87*
 Bethmale 21, 22
 Bidasoa (Bidassoa) *126-7*, **128**
 Biert 22
 Carança 15, 65, *66*, **67**
 Castelbó 23
 Cinca 107, *108*
 Fou 15
 Frau **18-9**, 20, *80*, **81**
 Freser *68-9*, 70
 Holzarte 33
 Kakouetta 33
 Madriu *74-5*, **76**
 Marcadau 103, *104-5*
 Monestero **88-9**, *89*
 Mourgouillou 77, *78-9*
 Nivelle 36
 Noguera Pallaresa **22**, 23
 Núria *68-9*
 Ossoue **26-7**, *98*, **99**
 Pineta 29, 30, **106-7**, *108*

Ribaouto 22
Riutort *87*
Sant Aniol 58, 59, *60*, **62**
Segré 16, 17
Soulcem 21, 82, **83**
Tech 15
Ustou 22
Vellos (Bellos) 29, 109, *110*
Yaga 30
Roncesvalles 33, 34, *120-1*
Roquefixade 18, 20
Roses 12, *48-9*, 50
Sadernes 14, 58, *60*, 61, **62**
St-Arroman 25
St-Aventin 26
St-Bertrand-de-Comminges 25, **26**
St-Etienne-de-Baïgorry 35, 36
St-Girons 21, 22
St-Jean-de-Luz 35, **36**
St-Jean-le-Vieux 33
St-Jean-Pied-de-Port 33, 34
St-Lizier 21, 22
St-Martin-du-Canigou **64**
Ste-Engrâce 33
Ste-Marie-de-Campan 26, 27, 28
Salardú 23
Saldes 16, 17
San Sebastián 35
Sant Joan de les Abadesses 14, 15
Sant-Miquel d'Engolasters **1**, **75**, *74-5*
Sant Miquel Sacot *55*, **56**, 57
Sant Pere de Rodes 12, **45**, *46-7*
Santa Pau 14, *55*, 57
Santesteban 35
Sare 36
Sarvisé 29
Seix 21, 22
Senterada 23, 24
La Seu d'Urgell 16, **17**, **73**
Talaixà **59**, *60*
Tarascon-sur-Ariège 18, 20, 21, 22
Tella 30
Thuès-entre-Valls 65, *66*, 67
Torla-Ordesa **29**, 30
Tour Madeloc **51**, *52-3*
Tuixén 16, 17
Urdos 32, *122*, 123, 124
Valcabrère 25
Vallfogona 15
Vera de Bidasoa *126-7*
Vicdessos 21
Vielha 23, 24
 Túnel de 23, 24
Vilajuïga 12, 45, *46-7*
Zuriza 32